Legal Aspects of Patient Confidentiality

Legal Aspects of Patient Confidentiality

Bridgit Dimond

QUAY
BOOKS

A division of MA Healthcare Ltd

Quay Books Division, MA Healthcare Ltd, St Jude's Church, Dulwich Road, London SE24 0PB

British Library Cataloguing-in-Publication Data
A catalogue record is available for this book

© MA Healthcare Limited 2010

ISBN-10: 1 85642 396 4
ISBN-13: 978 1 85642 396 0

Printed by CLE, Huntingdon, Cambridgeshire

Contents

Preface

This monograph follows the publication of a series of articles in the *British Journal of Nursing* on confidentiality. The need for a book for health professionals setting out the law and practice on confidentiality led to Quay Publications agreeing that the articles, updated and revised, could form the basis of a concise publication covering the main concerns which arise in respecting the duty of confidentiality. It is hoped that all registered health professionals (for convenience referred to here as practitioners) will find the book of value in their professional work, which involves the protection of the rights of the patient and working within the confines of the law. Trust is at the heart of the health professional/patient relationship, yet many practitioners find themselves in situations where they are torn between their duty of confidentiality to the patient and other duties. Knowledge of the law should assist them in resolving such dilemmas.

Acknowledgements

I would like to give my special thanks to Dr Yardley who read the entire typescript and made some valuable suggestions to the text, and who also recommended that the book should be marketed to other health professionals as well as nurses, since the issues considered here are important to them all. I should also record my considerable debt to Bette Griffiths in proofreading and preparing the indexes for the book and her constant encouragement and support.

CHAPTER I

The duty to respect patient confidentiality

Box 1.1 Case scenario: breach of confidentiality

Staff Nurse (S/N) Brown discovers that a recent admission on the surgical ward is a member of a famous pop band. She tells her friend, on a promise of total secrecy, that he has been admitted and will be having an operation for a hernia repair the following day. To her embarrassment and shame, the next day the papers publish the story and the disclosure is eventually traced to S/N Brown. What legal repercussions are likely and why?

The duty to respect patient confidentiality arises from a variety of sources including the duty of care to the patient, the contract of employment, professional codes of practice and Acts of Parliament.

Department of Health: Code of Practice on Confidentiality

The Department of Health published an NHS Confidentiality Code of Practice in 2003 (DH, 2003). This supersedes the earlier advice on the protection and use of patient information issued in 1996. The guidance covers the definition of confidentiality; providing a confidential service (including a confidentiality model); and using and disclosing confidential patient information. Annex A sets out the detailed requirements for providing a confidential service. Patients' health information and their interests must be protected through a number of measures, which include :

1. Recognising that confidentiality is an obligation for all staff, external contractors, and volunteers
2. Recording patient information accurately and consistently
3. Keeping patient information private
4. Keeping patient information physically and electronically secure
5. Disclosing information with appropriate care

Annex B sets out a model which can be used to aid decision making in disclosure situations. There are three distinct flow charts which distinguish three sets of circumstances:

■ B1, where it is proposed to disclose confidential information in order to provide healthcare
■ B2, where the purpose is not healthcare but it is a medical purpose as defined in legislation
■ B3, where the purpose is unrelated to healthcare or another medical purpose

Annex B states that these are important distinctions, in that the legal and ethical requirements differ in each case.

Duty of care to the patient

Implicit within the duty of care owed to the patient is the duty to recognise the right of the patient to have personal information relating to him/her kept confidential (*Furniss* v. *Fitchett* [1958]). In theory, therefore, the pop singer in the case scenario (see Box 1.1) could sue the employers of the nurse for their vicarious liability for the breach of confidentiality by the nurse. However, he is unlikely to do this since more publicity would be generated, when clearly he wished the admission to be kept secret. He would have to show that he suffered harm as a result of the disclosure if he were to rely upon an action for breach of the duty of care.

Often when royalty and other famous persons are admitted to hospital, their public relations officers agree with the hospital on an announcement of the admission and on the condition bulletins which are made during their stay. If, however, they wish for the admission and condition to be kept confidential, then this is their right. Had the singer been aware of the intent to publish before it actually took place, then he could have sought an injunction from the court to prevent the publication going ahead. An injunction is an order of the court prohibiting specified action taking place. Failure to comply with an injunction could lead to imprisonment for contempt of court. In the scenario the example of a pop singer is used, but of course the right to confidentiality applies to all patients and not just to the famous.

Duty under the contract of employment

Staff Nurse Brown could face disciplinary proceedings. It is either an express term (i.e. set out in writing or mentioned by word of mouth) of her contract of employment or an implied term (i.e. a term recognised by the courts as implicit within the contract of employment) that she should respect the confidential nature of information about patients. By failing to comply with this term of the contract of employment, she could be disciplined, the ultimate sanction being the loss of her job. Should she consider this to be an unfair dismissal, then if she has the requisite continuous service she could apply to the employment tribunal for a hearing. The employers would have to show the reason for the dismissal and the tribunal would decide if the employer acted reasonably in relying upon this reason to justify dismissal. (For further information on this see Dimond (2008).)

Duty of confidentiality arising from professional codes of practice

The NMC, the HPC and the GMC require all their registered practitioners to recognise the duty of confidentiality owed to the patient as part of the NMC Code of Professional Conduct (NMC, 2008).

The NMC in its 2008 Code states:

Respect people's confidentiality
■ You must respect people's right to confidentiality
■ You must ensure people are informed about how and why information is shared by those who will be providing their care
■ You must disclose information if you believe someone may be at risk of harm, in line with the law of the country in which you are practising

Under the duty to uphold the reputation of the profession, the NMC places the following duty on the registered practitioner:

You must cooperate with the media only when you can confidently protect the confidential information and dignity of those in your care

Additional guidance on confidentiality is given by the NMC in its advice sheet (NMC, 2009).

In August 2008 the HPC published guidance on confidentiality (HPC, 2008). It covers keeping information safe; disclosing information; disclosing information without consent; disclosing information by law; confidentiality; and accountability. It also provides a glossary. It will be referred to frequently in this book. Whilst it accepts that guidance cannot cover all situations, it lays down the following principles:

You should:
- take all reasonable steps to keep information about service users safe;
- get the service user's informed consent if you are passing on their information, and get express consent, in writing, if you are using the information for reasons which are not related to providing care or services for the service user;
- only disclose identifiable information if it is absolutely necessary, and, when it is necessary, only disclose the minimum amount necessary;
- tell service users when you have disclosed their information (if this is practical and possible);
- keep appropriate records of disclosure;
- keep up to date with relevant law and good practice;
- if appropriate, ask for advice from colleagues, professional bodies, unions, legal professionals or us [i.e. HPC]; and
- make your own informed decisions about disclosure and be able to justify them.

These principles for confidentiality are set out by the HPC in the context of the standards it has set on conduct, performance and ethics. These standards are shown in Box 1.2.

Box 1.2

1   You must act in the best interests of service users.
2   You must respect the confidentiality of service users.
3   You must keep high standards of personal conduct.
4   You must provide (to us and any other relevant regulators) any important information about your conduct and competence.
5   You must keep your professional knowledge and skills up to date.

6 You must act within the limits of your knowledge, skills and experience and, if necessary, refer the matter to another practitioner.

7 You must communicate properly and effectively with service users and other practitioners.

8 You must effectively supervise tasks you have asked other people to carry out.

9 You must get informed consent to give treatment (except in an emergency).

10 You must keep accurate records.

11 You must deal fairly and safely with the risks of infection.

12 You must limit your work or stop practising if your performance or judgement is affected by your health.

13 You must behave with honesty and integrity and make sure that your behaviour does not damage the public's confidence in you or your profession.

14 You must make sure that any advertising you do is accurate.

Whether or not S/N Brown loses her job, she could face professional conduct hearings before the NMC for her breach of the Code. It is likely that on the facts the NMC would consider disclosure of confidential information about a patient, without any lawful justification, to be misconduct by a nurse and evidence of unfitness to practise. It has various sanctions, the ultimate being removal from the register. If this is the outcome, then the nurse would lose her job. Other health professionals, such as psychologists (recently admitted as registered practitioners with the HPC), also have codes of conduct which require members to recognise the duty of confidentiality, and breach of this duty in circumstances where not justified could result in disciplinary action.

Duties arising from statutory provisions

Sometimes Acts of Parliament lay down clear provisions in relation to confidentiality and make breach of a duty of confidentiality a criminal offence. Thus, the Human Fertilisation and Embryology Act 1990 (as amended by the 1992 Act) makes stringent provisions on disclosure of information. (This is considered in Chapter 7 of this book.) Other statutes and regulations with penalties for breach of confidentiality include:

- Abortion Regulations 1991 (as amended in 2002) made under the Abortion Act 1967
- NHS (Venereal Disease) Regulations 1974
- The Data Protection Act 1998

None of these apply in S/N Brown's case. They are considered in later chapters of this book.

Human Rights Act 1998

The provisions of this Act came into force in England and Wales on 2 October 2000. They came into force on devolution in Scotland. The Act required all public authorities or organisations carrying out functions of a public nature to respect the European Convention of Human Rights, which is set out in Schedule 1 to the Act. In addition, it gave a right for citizens to bring an action in the courts of the UK if they considered that their human rights as set out in the Schedule had been breached by a public authority. Judges were also required to refer back to Parliament any legislation which they considered to be incompatible with the Articles set out in the European Convention of Human Rights.

One of the most significant changes brought about by this Act is that people no longer have to take their case to Strasbourg for a hearing before the European Court of Human Rights but can avoid the additional cost and delay and bring the case in local courts. If a judicial review is sought of a decision which is considered to be in breach of the human rights recognised in the Convention, then legal aid is available for this action. The House of Lords held that the definition of an organisation exercising functions of a public nature, for the purposes of the Human Rights Act, did not cover a care home under contract with local authorities for the provision of places (*YL* v. *Birmingham City Council* [2007]). As a consequence there was considerable concern that all those in private care homes would not have their human rights respected and the definition was amended by section 145 of the Health and Social Care Act 2008 which defines the provision of certain social care to be seen as a public function. Section 145 states that:

(1) A person ("P") who provides accommodation, together with nursing or personal care, in a care home for an individual under arrangements made with P under the relevant statutory provisions is to be taken for the purposes of subsection (3)(b) of section 6 of the Human Rights Act 1998 (c. 42) (acts of public authorities) to be exercising a function of a public nature in doing so.

Article 8 of the Convention states:

Everyone has the right to respect for his private and family life, his home and his correspondence.

2. There shall be no interference by a public authority with the exercise of this right except such as is in accordance with the law and is necessary in a democratic society in the interests of national security, public safety or the economic well-being of the country, for the prevention of disorder or crime, for the protection of health or morals, or for the protection of the rights and freedoms of others.

Paragraph 2 shows that the right to respect for private and family life is not absolute but qualified. Circumstances are specified where the article might not apply. The European Court has recognised the importance of preserving the confidentiality of medical records (Z. v. *Finland* 1998). The European Court of Human Rights decided that the refusal of the UK to amend its system of registering births so as to permit post-operative transsexuals to record their new sexual identity was not a breach of article 8 (*Sheffield* v. *UK* (1999)). Article 8 also has to be read in conjunction with article 10, which recognises a right to freedom of expression. Like article 8 this right is also qualified and if there were a conflict between one person's right to freedom of expression and another person's right to privacy, a judge would have to determine how those respective rights should be respected and the merits of each case. For example, a person might consider that a press account of their private life infringed their right to privacy. However, if that person was prominent in public life, proclaiming family values, yet supporting a mistress, the press might consider that freedom of expression was justified to expose such hypocrisy.

It is not clear how much additional protection this article adds to the duty of confidentiality in health care, but clearly privacy is a wider concept than confidentiality. For example, on a ward round a consultant might draw the curtains around a bed and then discuss the patient's diagnosis and treatment, talking in confidence to the multidisciplinary team and attempting to respect the principles of confidentiality. If, however, that conversation could be heard by others in the ward, it could be said that in practice there is a breach of confidentiality. In contrast, if a journalist saw a famous person being admitted to a psychiatric hospital and published an article on this, there would be no breach of confidentiality, since that information had not been obtained through any confidential disclosures. However, the publication would probably be a breach of article 8 and the person's respect for privacy unless publication could be justified under article 10 as part of the right of free expression. In the case of the model Naomi Campbell, the House of Lords in a majority decision held that even though she had brought into the public domain the fact that she was being treated for drug addition, certain information could still be kept confidential, including the time, form and place of the drug therapy, and she was therefore entitled to damages against the Mirror Group Newspapers for that breach of confidence (*Campbell* v. *MGN Ltd* [2004]). In this respect her right to privacy succeeded against the right to freedom of expression.

Access and human rights

Patients may be able to use certain articles to justify their obtaining access to their records. This issue is considered in Chapter 3.

Duty as part of the trust obligation between health professional and patient

In addition, the law recognises that there is a trust obligation between the health professional and the patient and, if there were to be an unauthorised disclosure, then the patient would have a remedy for this breach of trust. The pop singer in the case scenario (see Box 1.1) could therefore complain to the trust on this basis. S/N Brown has failed to respect the trust which she took on as a nurse.

Breach of trust by S/N Brown's friend

S/N Brown could claim that her friend failed to respect the confidentiality of the information which she had (wrongly) disclosed to her. This is also action-able. In the case of Stephens v. Avery and others [1988] (see Box 1.3) the claimant succeeded for breach of trust. In practice, of course, it is unlikely that S/N Brown would sue her friend. First, a basic principle in legal disputes is never to sue any person who is unlikely to be able to pay the compensation demanded; and, second, even if her friend obtained payment from the newspa-per for passing on that information and therefore had funds to pay compensa-tion, it is unlikely that the court would make an award which would result in the person guilty of the original disclosure benefiting from the profits of that disclosure.

Box 1.3 *Stephens* v. *Avery* and others [1988]

Unconscionable disclosure

The plaintiff and first defendant were close friends who freely discussed matters of a personal and private nature on the express basis that what the plaintiff told the first defendant was secret and disclosed in confidence. The first defendant passed on to the second and first defendants, who were the editor and publisher of a newspaper, details of the plaintiff's lesbian relationship with a woman who had been killed by her husband. The plaintiff brought an action against the defendants claiming damages on the grounds that the information was confidential and was knowingly published by the newspaper in breach of the duty of confidence owed by the first defendant to the plaintiff. In an action by the defendants to strike out the claim, since it showed no reasonable cause of action, the defendants failed and appealed to the Chancery Division. They lost on the grounds that, although the courts would not enforce a duty of confidence relating to matters which had a grossly immoral tendency, information relating to sexual conduct could be the subject of a legally enforceable duty of confidence if it would be unconscionable, for a person who had received information on the express basis that it was confidential, subsequently to reveal that information to another.

Remedies for enforcing the duty of confidentiality

If a person fears that information which has been disclosed in confidence is likely to be passed on to others, then an application can be made to the courts for an injunction to prevent the publication or disclosure of that information. Clearly, the advantage of this action is that it prevents the disclosure. Other remedies, which are available after the unjustified disclosure takes place, include an action for compensation for breach of contract (if the duty of confidentiality is contained in a contract) or an action in the tort of negligence for compensation for harm which has occurred. Mental harm would have to amount to a significant mental disorder for compensation to be payable. The court also has power to issue a declaration as to the rights of the claimant. Where the claim is brought under the Human Rights Act, then a declaration can be made that the disclosure is in breach of a specified article and the court can award compensation.

Disclosure with the consent of the patient

It is the right of the patient with the requisite mental capacity to give consent to any disclosure which would, without that consent, be a breach of confidentiality. A record that the patient had given consent would be good practice. However, it is important that there is an assessment that the patient has the requisite capacity to give consent. There is a presumption in law under the Mental Capacity Act 2005 that a person of 16 and over has the requisite mental capacity to make a specific decision, but that this presumption can be rebutted (i.e. removed) if there is evidence to the contrary. All the appropriate information should be given to the patient about the likely consequences of the disclosure before the patient gives consent. As for consent to treatment, the consent to disclosure should be voluntary, without fraud or coercion. Even when there are legal grounds for disclosing confidential information, it would still be good practice where possible and practicable to obtain the patient's consent to the disclosure. The confidentiality of information relating to children is considered in Chapter 10.

Disclosure in the best interests of the patient

Providing the reasonable standard of care and treatment required by law usually means that health information has to be passed amongst members of the multidisciplinary team caring for the patient. It would, for example, be a breach of the duty of care if a nurse were to fail to tell a doctor that the patient was allergic to a particular medicine, with the result that the patient was given medication which caused a severe reaction in the patient. Were the patient to sue for compensation in such circumstances it would be no defence for the nurse to assert that the patient did not give express consent for her to tell the doctor. Who makes up the multidisciplinary team? The actual composition will vary according to the patient's condition, but it may well include, as well as health professionals, social workers and other local authority (LA) employees. The team caring for the patient may also include complementary or alternative therapists. For example, a patient admitted for back pain may have been receiving treatment from an acupuncturist or reflexologist and it might be important for the health team to exchange information with that therapist to ensure that the treatments are compatible. Usually the patient's consent to such disclosure would be obtained, but it may be argued by other clinicians that if this consent were not given, he or she could not continue to treat the patient in ignorance of possibly vital information.

In some circumstances voluntary helpers may also have to be given information to ensure that the patient is safe. For example a volunteer taking a client with learning disabilities horse riding would need to know that the client suffers from epilepsy, so that the volunteer could be trained in how to deal with a fit. Such information is necessary in the best interests of the client. However, it would be a breach of confidentiality to inform the volunteer that the client had had an abortion five years before because that would not be in the best interest of the client, since it was irrelevant to the volunteer's activities with the client.

Best practice would be for whoever in the team has first contact with the patient to advise the patient that information he or she gives will be shared amongst the team and to obtain consent to that communication. However if the patient refused to consent, then that could prejudice the treatment which was provided. The Health Professions Council (2009) states in its guidance on confidentiality that:

> If you are using identifiable information to care for a service user or provide services to them, in most circumstances you will have their implied consent. Most service users will understand the importance of sharing information within the multidisciplinary team. If you are not sure whether you have implied consent, you should get express consent.

The NMC (2009) makes the following point in its guidance on confidentiality:

> Implied consent is obtained when it is assumed that the person in the care of a nurse or midwife understands that their information may be shared within the healthcare team. Nurses and midwives should make the people in their care aware of this routine sharing of information, and clearly record any objections.

Anonymous data

The duty of confidentiality applies to patient information from which the identity of the patient can be obtained, or which together with other information available to an individual identifies the patient. The Department of Health unsuccessfully claimed that rules of confidentiality applied to anonymous data. In the case of *R* v. *Department of Health ex p Source Informatics Ltd* [1999], the Department of Health challenged a data-collecting company that was using information provided by GPs and pharmacists about prescribing habits. The company believed the information would be useful to drug companies and would provide useful data for those interested in monitoring prescribing patterns. Even though the information would be anonymous, the Department of Health challenged the use of this information as a breach of the guidelines put forward by the Department of Health in (DH, 1996). It succeeded before the High Court but the Court of Appeal (*R* v. *Department of Health ex p Source Informatics Ltd* [2000]) reversed this decision. It held that GPs and pharmacists providing prescription information that did not identify the patient was not a breach of confidence. Anonymous data did not involve a risk to the patient's privacy, even if, with effort, the patient could be identified. The Court of Appeal was not prepared to allow the law of confidence to be distorted for the DH's purpose and suggested that if the DH continued to view such schemes as operating against the public interest, then it must take further powers in this already heavily regulated area to control or limit their effect. The DH did not appeal to the House of Lords.

Conclusion

The duty of confidentiality derives from various sources which act in parallel. Any case of unauthorised disclosure and breach of confidentiality could give rise to different proceedings, all considering different aspects of the situation: employment duties, professional duties and criminal offences. The rights set out in the European Convention relating to a right to respect for private and family life, home and correspondence may increase the number of cases where it is argued that there has been a failure to respect the duty of confidentiality. This may widen the basis of claims. The best practice is to obtain the patient's consent to any disclosure of confidential information. However, where this is lacking there are situations recognised in both statute and common law where the patient's refusal can be overridden. It is often confusing to the practitioner what circumstances justify disclosure, and it is to this difficult area that we turn in subsequent chapters.

References

Abortion (Amendment) (England) Regulations SI 2002 No 887.
Campbell v. *MGN Ltd* [2004] UKHL 22, [2004] 2 A.C. 457 HL.

Department of Health HSG (1996) 18: *Protection and Use of Patient Information*, DH circular, March 1996 (superseded by Department of Health, NHS Confidentiality Code of Practice, 2003.

Department of Health, NHS Confidentiality Code of Practice, 2003 available at http://www.dh.gov.uk/en/Managingyourorganisation/Informationpolicy/Patientconfidentialityandcaldicottguardians/DH_4100550 (superseding HSG(96) 18 LASSL (96)5).

Dimond, B. (2008) *The Legal Aspects of Nursing*, 5th edn. Pearson, Harlow.

Furniss v. *Fitchett* [1958] NZLR 396.

Health Professions Council (2008) *Confidentiality – Guidance for Registrants*. HPC, London.

Nursing and Midwifery Council (2009) *Advice Sheet: Confidentiality (A to Z Guidance)*. NMC, London.

Nursing and Midwifery Council (2008) *The Code: Standards of Conduct, Performance and Ethics for Nurses and Midwives*. NMC, London.

R v. *Department of Health ex p Source Informatics Ltd* [1999] EWCA Civ 3011 [1999] Lloyd's Rep Med 264, [1999] 4 All ER 185.

R v. *Department of Health ex p Source Informatics Ltd* [2000] TLR 17, [2000] 1 All ER 786 CA.

Sheffield v. *UK* [1999] 27 EHRR 163.

Stephens v. *Avery and others* [1988] 2 All ER 477.

YL v. *Birmingham City Council* [2007] UKHL 22; The Times 21 June 2007.

Z. v. *Finland* [1998] 25 EHRR 371.

CHAPTER 2

Disclosure of information in the public interest

Box 2.1 Case scenario

Staff Nurse (S/N) Black was a district nurse in a deprived inner city area. While visiting one family she realised that piled up in the corner of the living room were boxes of DVD players. She commented on them to the patient who became flushed and said that her husband was a trader and brought some of the stock home. S/N Black was convinced that they were stolen goods and decided that it was her duty as a good citizen to report this to the police. What is the law?

In the first chapter the sources of the duty of confidentiality were considered and it was noted that the health professional is bound to recognise the duty to protect all confidential information about the patient. This duty, however, is subject to specific exceptions. These exceptions include the following:

- Disclosure with the consent of the patient (see Chapter 1).
- Disclosure in the best interests of the patient (e.g. between members of the multidisciplinary team caring for the patient. This raises additional issues as to who belongs to the multidisciplinary team) (see Chapter 1).
- Disclosure as required by the court (see Chapter 4).
- Disclosure as required by statute (see Chapters 5, 7, 10, 11 and 14)
- Disclosure in the public interest (see this chapter)

This chapter discusses one of the most difficult exceptions to the duty of confidentiality: that of disclosure in the public interest. All health registration bodies and the Department of Health recognise that one of the main exceptions to the duty of confidentiality is disclosure in the public interest.

Guidance from the Nursing and Midwifery Council (NMC)

In its advice on confidentiality, the NMC (2009) states:

> The term 'public interest' describes the exceptional circumstances that justify overruling the right of an individual to confidentiality in order to serve a broader social concern.
>
> Under common law, staff are permitted to disclose personal information in order to prevent and support detection, investigation and punishment of serious crime and/or to prevent abuse or serious harm to others. Each case must be judged on its merits. Examples could include disclosing information in relation to crimes against the person e.g. rape, child abuse, murder, kidnapping, or as a result of injuries sustained from knife or gun shot wounds.

The NMC points out that the decisions are complex and must take account of both the public interest in ensuring confidentiality and the public interest in disclosure. The NMC states that:

> Disclosures should be proportionate and limited to relevant details.

> Registrants are advised to keep a clear record of the decision making process and the advice sought.

Guidance from the Health Professions Council (HPC)

The HPC gives the following guidance in its Confidentiality Guidance to Registrants issued in 2008:

Public interest
You can disclose confidential information without consent if it is in the public interest to do so. This might be in circumstances where disclosing the information is necessary to prevent a serious crime or serious harm to other people. You can find out whether it is in the public interest to disclose information by considering the possible risk of harm to other people if you do not pass it on, compared with the possible consequences if you do. This includes taking account of how disclosing the information could affect the care, treatment or services you provide to the service user.

You should carefully consider whether it is in the public interest to disclose the information. You should speak to your employer (if you have one). You may also want to get legal advice. You may be asked to justify a decision to disclose information in the public interest (or a decision not to disclose information) so it is important that you keep clear records.

You should still take appropriate steps to get the service user's consent (if possible) before you disclose the information. You should keep them informed about the situation as much as you can. However, this might not be possible or appropriate in some circumstances, such as when you disclose information to prevent or report a serious crime.

Guidance from the Department of Health

In its document *Confidentiality: a Code of Practice* (DH, 2003), the DH gives advice on disclosure in the public interest. It states that:

30. Under common law, staff are permitted to disclose personal information in order to prevent and support detection, investigation and punishment of serious crime and/or to prevent abuse or serious harm to others where they judge, on a case by case basis, that the public good that would be achieved by the disclosure outweighs both the obligation of confidentiality to the individual patient concerned and the broader public interest in the provision of a confidential service.

31. Whoever authorises disclosure must make a record of any such circumstances, so that there is clear evidence of the reasoning used and the circumstances prevailing. Disclosures in the public interest should also be proportionate and be limited to relevant details. It may be necessary to justify such disclosures to the courts or to regulatory bodies and a clear record of the decision making process and the advice sought is in the interest of both staff and the organisations they work within.

32. Wherever possible the issue of disclosure should be discussed with the individual concerned and consent sought. Where this is not forthcoming, the individual should be told of any decision to disclose against his/her wishes. This will not be possible in certain circumstances, e.g. where the likelihood of a violent response is significant or where informing a potential suspect in a criminal investigation might allow them to evade custody, destroy evidence or disrupt an investigation.

33. Each case must be considered on its merits. Decisions will sometimes be finely balanced and staff may find it difficult to make a judgement. It may be necessary to seek legal or other specialist advice (e.g.
from professional, regulatory or indemnifying bodies) or to await or
seek a court order. Staff need to know who and where to turn to for
advice in such circumstances.

34. Similarly, when the public good that would be served by disclosure
is significant, there may be grounds for disclosure. The key principle
to apply here is that of proportionality. Whilst it would not be reasonable and proportionate to disclose confidential patient information to a
researcher where patient consent could be sought, if it is not practicable
to locate a patient without unreasonable effort and the likelihood of
detriment to the patient is negligible, disclosure to support the research
might be proportionate. Other factors e.g. ethical approval, servicing
and safeguards, anonymisation of records and/or clear deletion policies
etc might also influence a decision on what is proportionate. It is important not to equate 'the public interest' with what may be 'of interest' to
the public.

The DH considers that serious harm, which would include murder, manslaughter, rape, treason, kidnapping, child abuse or other cases where individuals have suffered significant harm, may warrant breaching confidentiality.
Serious harm to the security of the state or to public order and crimes that
involve substantial financial gain or loss will also generally fall within this
category. In contrast, theft, fraud or damage to property where loss or damage
is less substantial would generally not warrant breach of confidence. The DH
refers to the definition of serious harm used by the GMC in an earlier publication as:

> a crime that puts someone at risk of death or serious harm and would
> usually be crimes against the person, such as abuse of children

A risk of harm would also be included within the definition of public interest. The DH gives the example of the risk of child abuse or neglect, assault, a
traffic accident or the spread of an infectious disease as being perhaps the most
common that staff may face.
In its advice in 2009 the GMC states that

> There is no agreed definition of 'serious crime'. *Confidentiality: NHS
> Code of Practice* (Department of Health, 2003) gives some examples of
> serious crime (including murder, manslaughter, rape and child abuse;
> serious harm to the security of the state and public order and 'crimes
> that involve substantial financial gain or loss' are mentioned in the same

category). It also gives examples of crimes that are not usually serious enough to warrant disclosure without consent (including theft, fraud, and damage to property where loss or damage is less substantial).

The DH points out:

> However, consideration of harm should also inform decisions about disclosure in relation to crime. Serious fraud or theft involving NHS resources would be likely to harm individuals waiting for treatment. A comparatively minor prescription fraud may actually be linked to serious harm if prescriptions for controlled drugs are being forged. It is also important to consider the impact of harm or neglect from the point of view of the victim(s) and to take account of psychological as well as physical damage. For example, the psychological impact of child abuse or neglect may harm siblings who know of it in addition to the child concerned.

Child abuse

From the guidance provided by the DH, the HPC and other registration bodies there is clearly no dispute that disclosure in the public interest must include protecting children. Therefore, if it comes to the notice of a practitioner that a child is being or is likely to be abused, whether physically, sexually or emotionally, then there would be a duty to report this to the appropriate person or organisation. This would be the person identified within the area child protection procedures. The NMC recommends that before any disclosure is made nurses and midwives should always discuss the matter fully with other professional colleagues and, if appropriate consult the NMC or their professional body or trade union. The NMC states that it is important that nurses and midwives are aware of their organisational policies and how to implement them. It advises that if disclosure takes place without the person's consent they should be told of the decision to disclose and a clear record of the discussion and decision should be made.

Serious harm to another person

If there is a reasonable fear that a person could cause physical harm to another, then this would probably be a justification for disclosure in the public interest.

This was the subject of a dispute in a decided case where a psychiatric patient argued that the report of a medical examination which he had requested from an independent psychiatrist should not have been disclosed to others (see the case of *W*. v. *Egdell* shown in Box 2.2).

Box 2.2 Case example: *W. v. Egdell* [1989]

'W' was detained in a secure hospital under section 37/41 of the Mental Health Act 1983 following a conviction for manslaughter on the grounds of diminished responsibility. He had shot dead five people and two others required major surgery. He applied to a Mental Health Review Tribunal for discharge or transfer to a regional secure unit with a view to his eventual discharge. His responsible medical officer supported his application but it was opposed by the Secretary of State. W obtained an independent medical report from Dr Egdell who strongly opposed his transfer. In the light of this report W withdrew the application to the tribunal. Dr Egdell had assumed that this report would be made available to the hospital and the tribunal. He sought the permission of W to place his report before the hospital but was refused permission. Dr Egdell then sent the report to the managers asking them to forward a copy to the Home Secretary since he considered that his examination had cast new light on the dangerousness of W and it ought to be known to those responsible for his care and for the formulation of any recommendations for discharge.

Subsequently, the Home Secretary referred W to a Mental Health Review Tribunal. The Home Secretary sent a copy of Dr Egdell's report to the tribunal. W then issued writs against Dr Egdell, the hospital board, the Home Secretary and the Secretary of State for Health and the tribunal, seeking injunctions preventing the defendants from using this material and claiming damages for breach of confidentiality. The trial judge held that the court had to balance the interest to be served by non-disclosure against the interest served by disclosure. Since W was not an ordinary member of the public but a detained patient in a secure unit, the safety of the public should be the main criterion. Dr Egdell had a duty to the public to place the result of his examination before the proper authorities, if in his opinion, the public interest so required. The public interest in disclosure outweighed W's private interest.

The Court of Appeal supported this reasoning and stated: 'A consultant psychiatrist who becomes aware, even in the course of a confidential relationship, of information which leads him, in the exercise of what the court considers a sound professional judgment, to fear that

> such decisions may be made on inadequate information and with a real risk of consequent danger to the public, is entitled to take such steps as are reasonable in the circumstances to communicate the grounds of his concern to the responsible authorities' (Lord Justice Bingham).

The ruling of the Court of Appeal in this case could apply to situations where a person discloses information to a nurse which indicates that others are at serious risk from that patient. Such a reasonable belief would justify the nurse in seeking to discuss this with senior managers and professional colleagues and in taking the appropriate action. The principle of disclosure in the public interest to prevent serious harm to others would also apply to situations of infectious disease, which would come under the notifiable diseases legislation.

Serious harm to the patient

What if a patient discloses that following a diagnosis of terminal illness he does not wish to continue to live but will end his life? While to attempt suicide is no longer a crime since the Suicide Act 1961, it is a crime to aid and abet another person to attempt to commit suicide. In the case of Diane Pretty, who was terminally ill with motor neurone disease, she lost her attempt to obtain a declaration from the court that it would be lawful for her husband to end her life so that she could die with dignity (*R. (Pretty)* v. *DPP* 2001). She also failed before the European Court of Human Rights. In contrast, Debbie Purdy won her case in the House of Lords when she argued that the Director of Public Prosecutions should clarify when there was likely to be a prosecution for aiding and abetting a suicide (*R. (Purdy)* v. *DPP* 2009). These cases are further discussed in Chapters 3 and 12).

It may be that the patient is profoundly depressed and could with appropriate counselling and assistance enjoy a good standard of life for his remaining time. There would, therefore, appear to be clear justification for the nurse to notify other professional persons who could offer the patient some assistance. Ideally, the nurse should attempt to obtain the patient's consent to this disclosure so that there is no breach of confidentiality. (This is further discussed in Chapter 12.) However, if the patient does not consent to the disclosure, passing on this information to others may be justified as being in the public interest to prevent serious harm to the patient. (This issue is considered in an article examining the ethics and law relating to suicide in the *End of Life Journal* by Rob George and B. Dimond (2009) (see Chapter 12).)

Serious criminal act

With regard to S/N Black in the case scenario of Box 2.1, are the circumstances which she faces sufficiently serious to justify disclosure in the public interest and do they place others at serious risk? There is no Act of Parliament which requires citizens to report their suspicions that a criminal act has been or is being committed, with the exception of acts of terrorism. The Prevention of Terrorism Acts (annually agreed) do require people to notify the police if they suspect activities relating to terrorism. Road traffic legislation requires the reporting of a road accident involving personal injuries or death. However, these are the only statutory requirements in relation to reporting crimes. If the test suggested by the HPC were applied to this situation S/N Black would have to ask herself what was the possible risk of harm to other people if she did not pass the information on, compared with the possible consequences if she did. There is likely to be very little harm to other people if she kept the information to herself, apart from the police not being warned of a possible crime and therefore more victims of theft arising. If she were to pass the information on, it could jeopardise her relationship with the family and care of the patient.

Nurses should not see their role as police informants. They should of course take appropriate action with suspected child abuse or other circumstances where there is a serious risk of personal injury. However, the situation which S/N Black encounters does not come within this category and therefore it does not come within the NMC's, HPC's or DH's definitions of public interest.

Benefit fraud

Similar difficulties of interpreting the 'public interest' exist in disclosure about benefit fraud: if a practitioner becomes aware that a family or individual is defrauding social security, should this be reported? The Government is appealing to individuals to notify agencies of evidence of such criminal behaviour. However, it is suggested that the practitioner's prime duty is to provide health care for the patient, and unless serious harm to a person is likely, then there is no justification for disclosure. It is always possible for legislation to be enacted which makes it a criminal offence not to make known reasonable suspicions of criminal conduct, including fraud, which would thereby radically change the role of the health professional. Such proposed legislation would probably be rigorously challenged by many health professionals.

Fitness to drive

Another example of the public interest exception to the duty of confidentiality is the reporting of a person's unfitness to drive to the DVLA.

The GMC states in its supplement to its guidance on confidentiality that it is in the public interest for patient confidentiality to be respected:

> However, there can also be a public interest in disclosing information:
>
> ■ to protect individuals or society from risks of serious harm, such as serious communicable diseases or serious crime;
> ■ or to enable medical research, education or other secondary uses of information that will benefit society over time.

> Personal information may, therefore, be disclosed in the public interest, without patients' consent, and in exceptional cases where patients have withheld consent, if the benefits to an individual or to society of the disclosure outweigh both the public and the patient's interest in keeping the information confidential. You must weigh the harms that are likely to arise from non-disclosure of information against the possible harm, both to the patient and to the overall trust between doctors and patients, arising from the release of that information.

> Disclosure of personal information about a patient without consent may be justified in the public interest if failure to disclose may expose others to a risk of death or serious harm. You should still seek the patient's consent to disclosure if practicable and consider any reasons given for refusal.

Reporting to the DVLA or DVA

The GMC advises that the Driver and Vehicle and Licensing Agency (DVLA) and Driver and Vehicle Agency (DVA) are legally responsible for deciding if a person is medically unfit to drive. This means they need to know if a driving licence holder has a condition or is undergoing treatment that may now, or in the future, affect their safety as a driver.

It recommends that:

> You should seek the advice of an experienced colleague or the DVLA or DVA's medical adviser if you are not sure whether a patient may be unfit to drive. You should keep under review any decision that they are fit, particularly if the patient's condition or treatments change. The DVLA's publication *For Medical Practitioners – At a glance Guide to*

the current Medical Standards of Fitness to Drive includes information about a variety of disorders and conditions that can impair a patient's fitness to drive.

4 The driver is legally responsible for informing the DVLA or DVA about such a condition or treatment. However, if a patient has such a condition, you should explain to the patient:
(a) that the condition may affect their ability to drive (if the patient is incapable of understanding this advice, for example, because of dementia, you should inform the DVLA or DVA immediately), and
(b) that they have a legal duty to inform the DVLA or DVA about the condition.

5 If a patient refuses to accept the diagnosis, or the effect of the condition on their ability to drive, you can suggest that they seek a second opinion, and help arrange for them to do so. You should advise the patient not to drive in the meantime.

6 If a patient continues to drive when they may not be fit to do so, you should make every reasonable effort to persuade them to stop. As long as the patient agrees, you may discuss your concerns with their relatives, friends or carers.

7 If you do not manage to persuade the patient to stop driving, or you discover that they are continuing to drive against your advice, you should contact the DVLA or DVA immediately and disclose any relevant medical information, in confidence, to the medical adviser.

8 Before contacting the DVLA or DVA you should try to inform the patient of your decision to disclose personal information. You should then also inform the patient in writing once you have done so.

Conclusion

The conclusion must be that S/N Black is probably in breach of her duty of confidentiality to the patient and the disclosure is not justified in the public interest. In theory, the family could complain to her employers, who may decide to take disciplinary action against her. If a prosecution against the family ensues, S/N Black could be called upon to give evidence. If she had decided not to inform the police, but the family were prosecuted anyway, she could still be called upon to give evidence in court. (This is considered in Chapter 4.)

Provisions relating to disclosure are contained in the Data Protection Act 1998 and it is to this we turn in the next chapter.

References

Department of Health (2003) *Confidentiality: NHS Code of Practice*. Available from http://www.dh.gov.uk/en/Publicationsandstatistics/Publications/PublicationsPolicyAndGuidance/DH_4069253.

General Medical Council (2009) *Guidance for Doctors: Confidentiality*. GMC, London.

George, R. and Dimond, B. (2009) Suicide: the legal and ethical aspects. *End of Life Journal*, **3**(4), 26–30.

Nursing and Midwifery Council (2009) *Advice Sheet: Confidentiality (A to Z Guidance)*. NMC, London.

Regina (Pretty) v. *Director of Public Prosecutions*, Secretary of State for the Home Department intervening The Times Law Report 5 December 2001; [2001] UKHL 61; [2001] 3 WLR 1598; [2002] 1 All ER 1; *Pretty* v. *UK* [2002] ECHR 427.

R. (Purdy) v. *Director of Public Prosecutions* The Times Law Report 24 February 2009; *R. (Purdy)* v. *Director of Public Prosecutions* The Times Law Report 31 July 2009 HL.

W v. *Egdell* [1989] 1 All ER 1089; [1990] 1 All ER 835 CA.

CHAPTER 3

Statutory provisions: Data Protection Act 1998, Freedom of Information Act 2000 and Health and Social Care Act 2001

Box 3.1 Case scenario

Assistant director of patient services, Ron Grey RGN, was the liaison officer with a computer firm for the automated processing of all patient records. He was asked to explain to a group of nurses the significance of the Data Protection Act 1998 and the legal requirements in respect of access to and use of the computerised records.

Until the passing of the Data Protection Act 1998 there had been a clear distinction between the legal requirements relating to computerised patient records and records in manual form. The former came under the rules of the Data Protection Act 1984 and the latter under the Access to Health Records Act 1990. However, the Data Protection Act 1998 applies to patient records whether they are held in a manual form (if they are part of a relevant filing system) or computerised form. The Access to Health Records Act 1998 has therefore been repealed except in the provisions relating to the records of those who have died (see below). The 1998 Act resulted from the European Directive (95/46/EC) which was designed to give further protection to individuals on the processing of personal data and on the free movement of such data. The Department of Health has provided advice and guidance on the legislation. (Department of Health, 2000; see Appendix 1 of this book). Information is also available from the website of the Information Commissioner (http://www.ico.gov.uk/).

The 1998 Act slightly amends the data protection principles (Table 3.1). The principles are further explained in part 2 of schedule 1 to the 1998 Act. Schedules 1, 2 and 3 relate to the basic principles and the processing of personal

Table 3.1 Data protection principles 1998.

1. Personal data shall be processed fairly and lawfully and, in particular, shall not be processed unless:
   a. at least one of the conditions in schedule 2 is met; and
   b. in the case of sensitive personal data, at least one of the conditions in schedule 3 is also met

2. Personal data shall be obtained only for one or more specified and lawful purpose, and shall not be further processed in any manner incompatible with that purpose or those purposes

3. Personal data shall be adequate, relevant and not excessive in relation to the purpose or purposes for which they are processed

4. Personal data shall be accurate and, where necessary, kept up to date

5. Personal data processed for any purpose or purposes shall not be kept for longer than is necessary for that purpose(s)

6. Personal data shall be processed in accordance with the rights of data subjects under the 1998 Act

7. Appropriate technical and organisational measures shall be taken against unauthorised or unlawful processing of personal data and against accidental loss or destruction of, or damage to, personal data

8. Personal data shall not be transferred to a country or territory outside the European economic area unless that country or territory ensures an adequate level of protection for the rights and freedoms of data subjects in relation to the processing of personal data

data, e.g. contractual purposes; compliance with a legal obligation; protection of the vital interests of the data subject; the administration of justice; the exercise of functions of the Crown or government department or other functions of a public nature; or meeting the legitimate interests of the data controller or a third party. These Schedules are included as appendices to the Department of Health circular which can be found in Appendix 1 to this book.

Records relating to physical or mental health come within the definition of sensitive personal data. One of Schedule 3 conditions must be satisfied. These conditions include:

■ The explicit consent of the data subject.
■ The use of the data is necessary to protect the vital interests of the data subject of another person and consent cannot be given by or on behalf of the data subject. (This situation would obviously cover records relating to the mentally incapacitated adult and children.)

■ The use of the data is necessary for medical purposes (including the purposes of preventive medicine, medical diagnosis, medical research, the provision of care and treatment and the management of healthcare services) and is undertaken by a health professional or a person who owes a duty of confidentiality which is equivalent to that which would arise if that person were a health professional.

Some of the terms used in the Data Protection Act 1998 are given different definitions from those used in the 1984 Act. The data subject has the same meaning as under the 1984 Act, i.e. 'the individual who is the subject of personal data'.

The data protection registrar, who is the national officer responsible for the oversight of the implementation of the law, is now known as the commissioner (as Information Commissioner he is responsible for the oversight of both the Data Protection Act 1998 and also the Freedom of Information Act 2000).

The data controller (formerly known as the data user) is the person who determines the purposes for which and the manner in which any personal data are to be processed.

Data now includes manually held records if they form part of a 'relevant filing system'. This means that the set is structured by reference to individuals so that specific information relating to a particular individual is readily accessible. The Court of Appeal considered the meaning of 'relevant filing system' in the case of *Durant* v. *Financial Services Authority* [2003] and held that the Act intended to cover manual files

only if they are of sufficient sophistication to provide the same or similar ready accessibility as a computerised filing system.

The Court of Appeal stated that

a 'relevant filing system' for the purposes of the Act, is limited to a system:

1) in which the files forming part of it are structured or referenced in such a way as to clearly indicate at the outset of the search whether specific information capable of amounting to personal data of an individual requesting it under section 7 is held within the system and, if so, in which file or files it is held; and

2) which has, as part of its own structure or referencing mechanism, a sufficiently sophisticated and detailed means of readily indicating whether and where in an individual file or files specific criteria or information about the applicant can be readily located.

Table 3.2 Rights of the data subject under the Data Protection Act 1998.

1. Right of subject access (sections 7–9)
2. Right to prevent processing likely to cause damage or distress (section 10)
3. Right to prevent processing for direct marketing purposes (section 11)
4. Right in relation to automated decision taking (section 12)
5. Right to take action for compensation if the individual suffers damage by any contravention of the Act by the data controller (section 13)
6. Right to take action to rectify, block, erase or destroy inaccurate data (section 14)
7. Right to make a request to the commissioner for an assessment to be made as to whether any provision of the Act has been contravened (section 42)

Further explanation of 'relevant filing system' is given by the Information Commissioner (2006) in his briefing note on the Durant case.

It is possible that notes kept of clinical supervision sessions by a supervisor which are not filed but kept in date order would not be seen as being in a 'relevant filing system' and would not therefore come under the provisions of the Data Protection Act.

The rights of the individual under the 1998 Act are shown in Table 3.2.

Section 30 enables the Secretary of State to draw up specific provisions relating to personal data of physical or mental health or condition of the data subject. The Secretary of State can exempt such data from subject information provisions. This is similar to the 1984 Act and the statutory instrument relating to access to health records. The statutory instrument for the 1998 Act is shown in Appendix 2. Access is excluded if serious harm to the physical or mental health or condition of the applicant or another person could be reasonably foreseen.

Information Commissioner

The Information Commissioner (formerly known as the Data Protection Commissioner) has the responsibility for promoting good practice and observance of the laws, for providing an information service and for encouraging the development of codes of practice and covers both the Data Protection legislation and the Freedom of Information Act. The Commissioner has considerable powers of enforcement under parts 3 and 5 of the Act. These include the power to serve enforcement notices and of entry and inspection. Offences under the Act are:

- Offences relating to failure to notify the commissioner or comply with his requests
- Unlawfully obtaining personal data
- Unlawful selling of personal data
- Forcing a person to compel access
- Unlawful disclosure of information by the commissioner/staff or agent

Case scenario

What specific advice can be given to Ron in the case scenario (Box 3.1)? First, in preparation for his role, Ron must obtain from the website of the Information Commissioner (http://www.ico.gov.uk/) an explanatory guide to the legislation. He could then discuss with the officer designated as data controller within his organisation the details of the registration under the Act and the process by which the records are to be placed on computer and a code of practice for ensuring that the data protection principles are followed in the organisation. He will agree with the computer firm and the senior management levels of access and passwords so that unauthorised persons cannot have access to the records. He will also ensure that records which are not to be placed on the computer, but will continue to be manually held, will also be subject to the same restrictions of access.

He will then ensure that staff attend training sessions, not only on how to use the computerised system, but also to help them understand the principles of the Data Protection Act. They need to know that it is a criminal offence to breach these principles and that they have a clear duty to protect patient confidentiality and prevent unauthorised access. He will also make contact with the NHS Board member who is designated as the Caldicott Guardian (see Chapter 8) and who has responsibilities for the security of information across the trust.

Ron will have to ensure that he keeps up to date with information from the Information Commissioner and with advice provided by the Department of Health. He must take steps to provide ongoing revision training and to ensure that registered practitioners understand, that like health and safety rules, confidentiality is not a subject which can be left to a single officer within the organisation. Each individual has a personal and professional responsibility to ensure that the law is implemented and that patients' rights are protected.

Access to records of dead patients

The only provisions of the Access to Health Records Act 1990 still valid are those applying to the records of dead patients. Section 3 (as amended by the Data Protection Act 1998 Schedule 16 Part 1) enables a personal representative of the patient or any person who may have a claim arising out of the patient's death to apply for access to his/her health records.

Personnel records

Under Data Protection legislation, employees also have the right to access their personnel files, whether they are in computerised format or held in manual files. A code of practice has been issued by the Information Commissioner on the use of personal data by employers which provides advice on the use of data in recruitment, references, appraisal, sickness records, medical and drug tests, email monitoring and phone use.

Access to Medical Reports Act 1988

This Act came into force on 1 January 1989. It gives an individual a right of access to any medical report relating to him or her which has been supplied by a medical practitioner for employment purposes or insurance purposes. Before any such medical report can be supplied, the individual must be notified that it is being requested and the individual must give consent to that request. The medical practitioner must not supply the report unless the consent of the individual has been given. He or she is also required to give the individual the opportunity of access to it and to be allowed to correct any errors. These provisions apply unless 21 days have elapsed since the practitioner notified the individual of his intention to provide a report. The medical report must be retained by the medical practitioner for at least six months from the date on which it was supplied.

There is an exemption from individual access where the medical practitioner is of the opinion that disclosure would be likely to cause serious harm to the physical or mental health of the individual or would indicate the intentions of the practitioner in respect of the individual or where the identity of another person would be made known.

Access to health records and the articles of European Convention

In addition to rights under the Data Protection Act access provisions, a patient may be able to claim that article 8 (see Chapter 1) entitles them to have access to their health records. In one case (*R* v. *Mid Glamorgan FHSA ex parte Martin* 1995) the Court of Appeal held that the patient did not have an absolute right to access records which had been created before the Access to Health Records Act came into force and that there had been no breach of article 8 of the European Convention of Human Rights. The doctor, however, had a duty to act in the best interests of the patient in deciding upon disclosure. In another case where the applicant was seeking access to his social services files (*Gaskin* v. *United Kingdom* 1989) the European Court of Human Rights held that article 8 had been breached because there was no system for independently reviewing whether access should be granted.

Health and Social Care Act 2001

Section 60 of the Health and Social Care Act 2001 gives to the Secretary of State powers to make, by regulations, provision for regulating the processing of prescribed patient information for medical purposes as he considers necessary or expedient:

- in the interests of improving patient care, or
- in the public interest.

The Regulations may make provision:

- for requiring prescribed communications of any nature which contain patient information to be disclosed by health service bodies in prescribed circumstances:
  - to the person to whom the information relates (where it relates to more than one person) to the person to whom it principally relates, or
  - to a prescribed person on behalf of any such person as is mentioned in sub-paragraph i. or ii.
- for requiring or authorising the disclosure or other processing of prescribed patient information to or by persons of any prescribed description subject to compliance with any prescribed conditions (including conditions requiring prescribed undertakings to be obtained from such persons as to the processing of such information)

■ for securing, that, where prescribed patient information is processed by a person in accordance with the regulations, anything done by him in so processing the information shall be taken to be lawfully done despite any obligation of confidence owed by him in respect of it

■ for creating offences punishable on summary conviction by a fine not exceeding level 5 on the standard scale or such other level as is prescribed or for creating other procedures for enforcing any provisions of the regulations.

Section 60 (3)–(7) place restrictions on the Regulations which can be made.

In spite of these limitations on the power to make regulations, these are extremely extensive powers given to the Secretary of State and much will depend upon the conditions which are laid down in the regulations.

The Regulations passed under the Act (SI 2002/1438) have enabled Cancer Registers to receive confidential patient information, and information about communicable diseases and other risks to public health can also be passed on under Regulation 3. Regulation 4 states that:

Anything done by a person that is necessary for the purpose of processing confidential patient information in accordance with these regulations shall be taken to be lawfully done despite any obligation of confidence owed by that person in respect of it.

This provides protection from any potential breach of confidentiality action if the Regulations have been complied with.

Regulation 5 and the Schedule to the Regulations enable confidential information to be processed for medical purposes provided that the processing has been approved, in the case of medical research, by the Secretary of State and a research ethics committee, and in any other case by the Secretary of State. The Schedule defines the circumstances in which this processing can take place.

For the purposes of section 60 patient information is defined as:

■ Information (however recorded) which relates to the physical or mental health or condition of an individual, to the diagnosis of this condition or to his care or treatment, and

■ Information (however recorded) which is to any extent derived directly or indirectly, from such information.

Such information is confidential if

■ the identity of the individual in question is ascertainable from that information or from that information and other information which is in the possession of, or is likely to come into the possession of, the person processing that information, and

■ that information was obtained or generated by a person who, in the circumstances, owed an obligation of confidence to that individual.

'Medical purposes' is defined to include preventative medicine, diagnosis, research, provision of care and treatment, the management of health and social care services and informing patients about diagnosis, treatment and care.

'Processing' means the use, disclosure or obtaining of the information or the doing of such other things in relation to it as may be prescribed.

Section 61 provided for the establishment of a Patient Information Advisory Group. This was subsequently abolished and replaced by the National Information Governance Board for Health and Social Care, which is discussed in Chapter 8.

An Ethics and Confidentiality Committee (ECC) has been established to undertake the responsibilities of the National Information Governance Board under section 251 of the NHS Act 2006 and to consider and advise on ethical issues relating to the processing of health or social care information as referred to it by the NIGB. Section 251 of the NHS Act 2006 (originally enacted under Section 60 of the Health and Social Care Act 2001), allows the common law duty of confidentiality to be set aside in specific circumstances where anonymised information is not sufficient and where patient consent is not practicable. Applications for approval to use Section 251 support (previously considered by the Patient Information Advisory Group (PIAG)) are now considered by the ECC.

NHS Care Record Guarantee (CRG)

The NHS Care Record Guarantee for England sets out the rules that govern how patient information is used in the NHS and what control the patient can have over this. It covers people's access to their own records, controls on others' access, how access will be monitored and policed, options people have to further limit access, access in an emergency, and what happens when someone cannot make decisions for themselves. Everyone who works for the NHS or for organisations delivering services under contract to the NHS has to comply with this guarantee. The guarantee was first published in 2005 and is regularly reviewed by the National Information Governance Board to ensure it remains clear and continues to reflect the law and best practice. Revisions were made in 2009 to include the changes as a result of the abolition of the Patient Information Advisory Group and the transfer of its functions to the NIGB as part of the Health and Social Care Act 2008. In answer to comments, it was made clear that:

- The CRG applies to both paper and electronic patient records;
- Both technology and business processes can be used to comply with the 12 commitments;
- The CRG applies to all staff who access patient records not just to health-care professionals; and
- Sample audits are appropriate when seeking to identify inappropriate access to records.

Freedom of Information Act 2000

The purpose of this Act is to provide a general right of access to information held by public authorities. However, personal information is regarded as exempt information and comes within the provisions of the Data Protection Act 1998. The two Acts work separately, so that applications for access to personal information must be made under the Data Protection Act 1998 (see section 40 Freedom of Information Act 2000). Under section 41 of the Freedom of Information Act 2000 information is exempt from the provisions of the Act if

- it was obtained by the public authority from any other person (including another public authority), and
- the disclosure of the information to the public (otherwise than under this Act) by the public authority holding it would constitute a breach of confidence actionable by that or any other person.

The full implementation of the Freedom of Information Act has led to a considerable number of applications to public authorities for access to information. If the information is refused by the organisation concerned the applicant can appeal to the Information Commissioner. His decisions are subject to appeal and a hearing before the Information Tribunal. The following is an example of a case heard under the Freedom of Information Act.

Bluck v. Information Commissioner (2007)

The mother of a girl who had died in hospital appealed against the decision of the Information Commissioner to refuse her access to her daughter's records. The trust was unwilling to release the records without the consent of the daughter's husband as her next of kin. The hospital had admitted liability for the daughter's death and had reached a settlement with the husband involving payment of substantial compensation. The mother contended that the records did not fall within the exception for confidential information under the Freedom of Information Act 2000 s. 41, since the trust would have the following defences to any breach of confidence claim arising from the disclosure: (1) the public interest in the disclosure of information in cases where a hospital had been negligent in its treatment of a patient, leading to the patient's death, outweighed the public interest in maintaining confidence; (2) neither the daughter nor her estate would suffer any detriment as a result of the disclosure; (3) a cause of action in breach of confidence could not survive the death of the person to whom the duty of confidence was owed; and (4) even if the cause of action did survive, the deceased's personal representative would not be entitled to bring an action to enforce the deceased's right to confidentiality in relation to medical records.

The Judge refused the application:

- The public interest ensuring that patients retained trust in confidentiality of information they gave to doctors outweighed, by some way, the countervailing public interest in disclosure of a deceased's medical records.
- If disclosure would be contrary to an individual's reasonable expectation of maintaining the confidentiality of his or her private information, then the absence of detriment in the sense contemplated by the mother was not a necessary ingredient of the cause of action.
- The duty of confidence was capable of surviving the death of the confider. The trust would be in breach of confidence owed to the daughter if it disclosed her medical records other than under the terms of the Act, and the breach would be actionable by the daughter's personal representatives. Her records were exempt information under S 41 and should not be disclosed.

The rights of the next of kin had to prevail where the rights and wishes of family members differed.

Conclusions

The Information Commissioner has a remit to monitor the implementation of the Data Protection and Freedom of Information legislation and his website is a valuable source of guidance. The implications of the replacement of the Patient Information Advisory Group by the National Information Governance Board for Health and Social Care are still to be ascertained.

References

Bluck v. *Information Commissioner* (2007) 98 B.M.L.R. 1.

Department of Health (2000) *Health Service Circular* 2000/009.

Gaskin v. *United Kingdom* (1989) 12 EHRR 36 (ECt HR).

Information Commissioner (2006) *The 'Durant' Case and its Impact on the Interpretation of the Data Protection Act 1998.* Available online at http://www.ico.gov.uk/upload/documents/library/data_protection/detailed_specialist_guides/the_durant_case_and_its_impact_on_the_interpretation_of_the_data_protection_act.pdf.

Michael John Durant v. *Financial Services Authority* [2003] EWCA Civ 1746, Court of Appeal (Civil Division).

R v *Mid Glamorgan FHSA ex parte Martin* [1995] 1 WLR 110 CA.

CHAPTER 4

Confidentiality and the courts

Box 4.1 Case scenario

Arthur Green, a physiotherapist at Roger Park Hospital, had been told by a patient, Dan Davies, that his injuries occurred when he was attempting to burgle a house and fell from a window. Arthur promised Dan that he would never disclose this information. Arthur is then summoned as a witness for the prosecution of Dan, who has pleaded not guilty to the offence. Arthur considers that Dan gave that information to Arthur because he trusted him and is reluctant to give evidence against Dan. What is the legal position?

Introduction

It is not always appreciated that there is no right or privilege for a nurse or doctor or other health professional to respect the confidentiality of information provided by the patient when the health professional is required to answer questions by a court of law. Even a priest would be legally bound to disclose information learned in the confessional if the judge considered that information given by the confessor was relevant to an issue arising in the court. This chapter looks at the extent and process by which the court can require a health professional to breach the duty of confidentiality.

Criminal cases

If the police require information from potential witnesses in a criminal investigation, then the witnesses have to answer the reasonable questions of the police, otherwise they would be guilty of a criminal offence. Where police wish to access personal health records then the provisions of the Police and Criminal Evidence Act 1984 apply. Under section 9, health records are excluded material and the police have to obtain permission from a circuit judge in accordance with the provisions of schedule 1 to the Act. Many police forces have developed policies with their local accident and emergency departments over accessing patient information. It is important to ensure that these do not exceed the lawful powers of the police and respect the duty of confidentiality owed to the patient. The patient can of course give consent to the disclosure, thus saving the police having to go through the procedure under the Police and Criminal Evidence Act. (This is considered in Chapter 14.)

Court hearing

In the above case scenario Arthur would have no right to refuse to give evidence in the prosecution of Dan Davies. A subpoena could be issued for him to attend court and give evidence. If he ignored this then a warrant could be issued for his arrest. If he obeyed the subpoena, but once in court refused to answer questions on the grounds that he would be breaching the confidentiality of the patient, then the judge has the power to commit him to prison until he has 'purged his contempt'.

In retrospect Arthur should never have made the promise to Dan. A health professional cannot promise a patient that certain information will be kept confidential whatever circumstances arise since the court can direct the disclosure of that information. It is preferable for the practitioner to make the patient aware before confidential information of a criminal nature might be disclosed that a guarantee of absolute secrecy cannot be given.

Exceptions to the judge's powers to require evidence to be given

Legal professional privilege

This covers confidential communications between clients and their legal advisers for the purpose of giving or receiving legal advice, and to any communications whose dominant purpose is the prosecution or defence of legal proceedings. The judge cannot order disclosure of such communications. The reason is that it is in the interests of justice for a client to be able to confide fully with legal advisers without fear that such communications would be ordered to be disclosed in court. Reports to legal advisers are also privileged from disclosure if the principal purpose for which they were written is in contemplation of litigation.

Sometimes there may be several purposes behind the preparation of a report, e.g. following a health and safety accident, where the report can be used for both management purposes in order to prevent a similar accident arising again and for legal purposes. This was the situation in the case of *Waugh* v. *British Railways Board* [1980]. In this case the House of Lords held that if the predominant purpose behind the report is for advice and use in litigation, then it will be privileged from disclosure. This ruling was applied in the case of *Lask* v. *Gloucester* [1985] (Box 4.2). In the Freedom of Information Act 2000 (see Chapter 3) the existence of legal professional privilege was recognised and supported. Section 42 of the Freedom of Information Act states that information in respect of which a claim to legal professional privilege or, in Scotland, to confidentiality of communications, could be maintained in legal proceedings is exempt information.

Box 4.2 Case: *Lask* v. *Gloucester* [1985]

The court applied the ruling in *Waugh* v. *British Railways Board* in the situation where the health authorities claimed legal professional privilege in respect of confidential reports completed following an accident. The court held that in spite of declarations by the health authorities and solicitors to this effect, the documents were not covered by legal professional privilege.

Public interest immunity

The other exception to the right of the judge to order disclosure of any document relevant to an issue before it, is that of public interest immunity. This covers such interests as the national security. The privilege from disclosure is given under the sworn affidavit of a minister and can be overruled by the judge. Public interest immunity was considered by the Scott Inquiry, which recommended that immunity certificates should not be issued in criminal proceedings, if the liberty of the subject was at stake.

Civil proceedings

Disclosure to the patient before litigation commences

In civil proceedings there is statutory provision in the Supreme Court Act 1981 for information to be made available before litigation actually commences and this information can include the detailed health records of the patient. If a client is suing in relation to an incident during care by a health professional his or her records could be ordered to be disclosed to the legal advisers or professional advisers of the patient. This right enables a potential claimant to have early access to the records to ascertain if litigation is justifiable.

Also, it is possible for the patient to obtain access to the records whether held in computer or manual form under the Data Protection Act 1998. However, there is no absolute right to access the records, and access can be withheld if serious harm could be caused to the mental or physical health of the applicant or another person, or if a third person identified in the records has requested that access should be withheld. (This latter exception does not apply if the third person is a health professional involved in the patient's care.) Fear of possible litigation would not be grounds for preventing patient access to the records.

The Woolf Reforms, which have aimed at speeding up the process of civil litigation, have emphasised the need for information to be made available between the parties before litigation commences and the judge in his or her new role as case manager has considerable powers to order the disclosure of information between the parties in the interests of justice (see Civil Procedure Rules, below). A preaction protocol has been set out with which parties must comply and sanctions are available if the times and requirements in the protocol are not met.

Access by the third party

Under section 34 of the Supreme Court Act 1981 disclosure can be ordered against a person who is not likely to be a party to the case. A possible situation where it would apply is shown in Box 4.3.

Confidentiality ordered by the courts

Where sensitive issues are involved, usually involving children and mentally incapable adults, the court has the power to order the press to refrain from mentioning the personal details of those involved in any case. In the case of the boys who were

> ## Box 4.3 Case situation: disclosure ordered against an NHS trust
>
> A former patient is involved in a road traffic accident and sues the driver of the vehicle which caused the accident. This driver wished to have access to information about the patient held by the trust relating to its care in order to determine the likely prognosis of the patient. If, for example, there was concern that the patient was unlikely to make a full recovery as a result of the road accident, but that he suffered from severe disabilities anyway, these existing disabilities could affect both liability of the driver and also the amount of compensation payable (quantum).

found guilty of killing James Bulger, whilst their names were disclosed early on in their trial, upon their release from custody, the judge granted blanket privacy on the grounds that 'they were seriously at risk of injury or death if their identities were disclosed' (*Venables & Anor* v. *News Group News Papers Ltd & Ors* [2001]). The extent of the injunction was subsequently reduced in scope because it was considered to be excessive in its range.

Civil Procedure Rules

Part 31 of the Civil Procedure Rules (CPR) cover the topics of discovery and inspection of documents. The Rules can be accessed on the Ministry of Justice or open government websites (http://www.open.gov.uk/lcd/civil/procrules_fin/crules.htm). A party discloses a document by stating that the document exists or has existed. Rule 31.16 covers the disclosure of documents before proceedings start. Where the applicant and respondent are likely to be parties to the proceedings, then the court can order disclosure if it is desirable in order to (i) dispose fairly of the anticipated proceedings; (ii) assist the dispute to be resolved without proceedings; or (iii) save costs.

Conclusion

In deciding whether disclosure of confidential information is appropriate there is, in a sense, a hierarchy of priorities. The needs of justice in courts of law, litigation and prosecutions come before the individual rights of a patient to have information kept confidential. Nurses should be aware of this important exception to the duty of confidentiality. The exception is recognised by the NMC, which in its advice on confidentiality states that:

> If a nurse or midwife is summoned as a witness in a court case he/she must give evidence. There is no special rule to entitle the nurse or midwife to refuse to testify. If a nurse or midwife refuses to disclose any information in response to any question put to him/her, then a judge may find the nurse or midwife in contempt of court and may ultimately send him/her to prison (NMC, 2009).

Other registration bodies also recognise this exception and provide advice accordingly. It is important that the individual practitioner should understand the extent and limitations of the courts and of the police to require disclosure.

References

Lask v. *Gloucester* [1985] The Times Law Report, 13 December; [1991] 2 Med. LR 379.

Nursing and Midwifery Council (2009) *Advice Sheet: Confidentiality (A to Z Guidance)*. NMC, London.

Venables & Anor v. *News Group News Papers Ltd & Ors* [2001] EWHC QB 32 (8 January 2001).

Waugh v. *British Railways Board* [1980] AC 521.

CHAPTER 5

The notification of infectious diseases

Box 5.1 Case scenario

Jenny Rose was a paediatric community nurse who regularly visited a child with a chronic lung condition who was being nursed at home. On one visit she noticed that the child's mother appeared to be very pale and thin and was told that the mother had a severe gastric disorder with diarrhoea. From the description of the illness, Jenny thought that Jane might be suffering from typhoid. Jane worked as a cook in a restaurant, was unwilling to seek medical advice and intended going to work that night. Jenny was concerned that Jane could have a serious notifiable infectious disease and therefore be a danger to customers in the restaurant. Jane insisted that Jenny should keep the information confidential. Where does Jenny stand?

Introduction

There are very few statutes which require information to be given to the police or other public authorities, but public health and the control of infectious diseases is one major exception.

Notifiable diseases

Diseases which are notifiable are shown in Box 5.2.

Box 5.2 Notifiable diseases

Category A: cholera, plague, relapsing fever, smallpox, typhus

Category B: acquired immune deficiency syndrome (AIDS) acute encephalitis, acute poliomyelitis, meningitis, meningococcal septicaemia, anthrax, diphtheria, dysentery, paratyphoid fever, typhoid fever, viral hepatitis, leprosy, leptospirosis, measles, mumps, rubella, whooping cough, malaria, tetanus, yellow fever, ophthalmia neonatorum, scarlet fever, tuberculosis, rabies and viral haemorrhagic fever

Category A covers those notifiable diseases which come under the duties set by the Public Health (Control of Disease) Act 1984. These diseases must be reported to the local authority. Those diseases under category B are covered by Regulation 3 of the Public Health (Infectious Diseases) Regulations 1988 (SI 1988 No 1546) and the 1984 Act applies to a more limited extent.

Procedure of notification

Under section 11 of the 1984 Act a registered medical practitioner has a duty to notify the proper office of the local authority if he or she becomes aware, or suspects, that a patient whom he or she is attending within the district of a local authority is suffering from a notifiable disease or from food poisoning. The duty does not apply if the practitioner believes, and has reasonable grounds for believing, that some other registered medical practitioner has complied with the duty.

What information must be notified? The information which must be given is shown in Box 5.3. The health authority must be notified within 48 hours of the local authority notification.

Powers of the justice of the peace

Because of the importance of safeguarding the public health, justices of the peace (JPs) are given statutory powers to intervene. For example, under section 37 of the Public Health (Control of Disease) Act 1984, the JP has the power

---

Box 5.3 Information which must be given (Public Health (Control of Disease) Act 1948 Section 11)

1. Name, age and sex of the patient and the address of the premises where the patient is;
2. the disease or, as the case may be, particulars of the poisoning from which the patient is, or is suspected to be, suffering and the date or approximate date of its onset; and
3. if the premises are a hospital, the day on which the patient was admitted, the address of the premises from which he came there and whether or not, in the opinion of the person giving the certificate, the disease or poisoning from which the patient is, or is suspected to be, suffering was contracted in hospital.

(NB: Section 11(4) imposes a criminal sanction on a person who fails to comply with an obligation imposed under the provisions set out above.)

---

to remove a person to hospital if satisfied that certain factors are present. The factors are that: a person is suffering from a notifiable disease; the sufferer's circumstances are such that proper precautions to prevent the spread of infection cannot be taken or that such precautions are not being taken; the risk of infection is thereby caused to other persons; and accommodation is available in a suitable hospital.

Under section 38 the JP can order the detention of a person suffering from a notifiable disease in a hospital for infectious diseases. Other provisions for Public Health (Control of Disease) Act 1984 are set out in Box 5.4.

Box 5.4 Other provisions of public health legislation

Section 13 gives the Secretary of State power to make regulations to prevent the spread of notifiable diseases and preventing dangers from the arrival or departure of aircraft or vessels.

Section 43 enables the registered medical practitioner to take precautions in order to prevent the spread of infection where a person suffering from a notifiable disease dies in hospital.

Section 44 requires the person in charge of the premises where a person with a notifiable disease has died to take precautions to prevent any one coming into contact with the body.

Section 47 enables the Secretary of State to make regulations relating to the disposal of dead bodies.

Section 48 allows JPs to make an order for the removal of a body and for burial within a specified time to prevent the lives of others being endangered.

Venereal disease provisions

Venereal diseases are one of the few conditions which have explicit statutory provisions covering confidentiality. The National Health Service (Venereal Diseases) Regulations 1974 place a duty on health authorities to ensure that any information capable of identifying an individual examined or treated for any sexually transmitted disease shall not be disclosed. The only exceptions to this duty of confidentiality are where the information must be communicated to a medical practitioner (or person employed under the direction of a medical practitioner) in connection with the treatment of persons suffering from such disease and for the purpose of such treatment or prevention.

The effect of this regulation is to impose extremely tight precautions against any unauthorised disclosure in genitourinary clinics and treatment centres. Such clinics should not pass any confidential information over the phone and should not even disclose information to the caller, unless there is clear evidence that the caller is the patient.

AIDS/HIV

Acquired immunodeficiency syndrome (AIDS)/ human immunodeficiency virus (HIV) was held to be a sexually transmitted disease for the purpose of the venereal disease regulations even though there are other ways in which the disease is transmitted (*X* v. *Y*, 1988). The notification provisions of the Public Health (Control of Disease) Act 1984 do not apply to AIDS. Under the AIDS (Control) Act 1987 (as extended by the 1988 Act) reports given to the Secretary of State on a number of persons who have tested positive to HIV.

Under the Public Health (Infectious Diseases) Regulations 1985, local authorities have been given the power to apply to a JP for the removal of an AIDS sufferer to hospital to be detained there. The JP is also given the power to make an order for a person believed to be suffering from AIDS to be medically examined. There are also powers in relation to the disposal of the body of an AIDS sufferer. Confidentiality in relation to AIDS/HIV is considered in Chapter 6.

Guidance from the General Medical Council

The GMC published in 2009 a supplementary paper to its Confidentiality Guidance covering the disclosure of information about serious communicable diseases (GMC, 2009). It quotes from the Confidentiality Guidance, emphasising the fact that confidentiality is central to trust between doctors and patients and without assurances about confidentiality, patients may be reluctant to seek medical attention or to give doctors the information they need in order to provide good care. However, appropriate information sharing is essential to the efficient provision of safe, effective care, both for the individual patient and for the wider community of patients.

It therefore advised its registered members that:

You must disclose information to satisfy a specific statutory requirement, such as notification of a known or suspected case of certain infectious diseases.

There is a clear public good in having a confidential medical service. The fact that people are encouraged to seek advice and treatment, including for communicable diseases, benefits society as a whole as well as the individual. Confidential medical care is recognised in law as being in the public interest. However, there can also be a public interest in disclosing information: to protect individuals or society from risks of serious harm, such as serious communicable diseases or serious crime; or to enable medical research, education or other secondary uses of information that will benefit society over time.

Personal information may, therefore, be disclosed in the public interest, without patients' consent, and in exceptional cases where patients have withheld consent, if the benefits to an individual or to society of the disclosure outweigh both the public and the patient's interest in keeping the information confidential. You must weigh the harms that are likely to arise from non-disclosure of information against the possible harm, both to the patient and to the overall trust between doctors and patients, arising from the release of that information.

Disclosure of personal information about a patient without consent may be justified in the public interest if failure to disclose may expose others to a risk of death or serious harm. You should still seek the patient's consent to disclosure if practicable and consider any reasons given for refusal.

Its Supplementary guidance states that

Confidentiality is important to all patients. Those who have, or may have, a serious communicable disease might be particularly concerned about their privacy. You should make sure that information you hold or control about a patient's infection status is at all times effectively protected against improper disclosure. All patients are entitled to good standards of care, regardless of their status, what disease they might have, or how they acquired it.

Its advice on Good Medical Practice states that:

You should protect your patients, your colleagues and yourself by being immunised against common serious communicable diseases where vaccines are available.

If you know that you have, or think that you might have, a serious condition that you could pass on to patients, or if your judgement or performance could be affected by a condition or its treatment, you must consult a suitably qualified colleague.

You must ask for and follow their advice about investigations, treatment and changes to your practice that they consider necessary. You must not rely on your own assessment of the risk you pose to patients.

Jenny's situation

It is of course pure chance that Jenny has come across a possible case of infectious disease. Jane is not her patient. Jenny only suspects that Jane may have a notifiable and infectious disease; she does not know for sure. However, since Jane works in the catering industry, if Jenny keeps quiet the public's health may be at risk. Ideally, Jenny should try to persuade Jane to seek medical advice, but she could warn her that if Jane fails to take action then Jenny herself would ensure that Jane's GP or the local authority was notified. However, it should be made clear that Jenny does not have a statutory duty to notify the local authority of the possibility of the disease. If she were to pass on the information to the appropriate sources then she would have to rely upon the justification that the disclosure was in the interests of public safety. Disclosure in the public interest was considered in the second chapter of this book. It is important that Jenny keeps clear comprehensive records of the reasons why she discloses any confidential information and to whom she makes the disclosure.

Health and Social Care Act 2008

In the wake of the swine flu outbreak, increased power has been given to the Secretary of State to control infection or contamination and protect the public health. Part 3 of the Health and Social Care Act Section 129 adds new sections 45A–45T to the Public Health Act 1948 enabling regulations to be made to provide greater control over public health.

Section 76 of the 2008 Act creates a criminal offence if information obtained by the Care Quality Commission (which has been obtained in confidence and which identifies a person) is knowingly or recklessly disclosed. Section 77 provides defences to the charge including the fact that the disclosure was with the consent of the person concerned, or the individual could not be identified, or that the disclosure was necessary or expedient for the purpose of protecting the welfare of any individual.

Section 79 sets out the circumstances in which the CQC is permitted to make disclosures of confidential information. The CQC is required to prepare and publish a code in respect of the practice it proposes to follow in relation to confidential personal information (s. 80).

Conclusions

Disclosure of information to protect public health is an example of the duty of confidentiality being set aside in the public interest. The AIDS/HIV patient presents considerable dilemmas in relation to confidentiality and it is to this that we turn in the next chapter.

References

General Medical Council (2009) *Confidentiality: Disclosing Information About Serious Communicable Diseases.* GMC, London.

X v. *Y* [1988] 2 All ER 648.

CHAPTER 6

HIV/AIDS patients and the duty of confidentiality

Box 6.1 Case scenario

Staff Nurse Grey discovered that one of the junior doctors in the medical team was human immunodeficiency virus (HIV) positive. She felt that she was under a duty to disclose this information in order that the patients could be protected from cross-infections. Since her senior manager appeared to take little notice of the information, she informed the press. What is the law?

Introduction

The spread of human immunodeficiency virus (HIV) infection across the country is still proceeding and research suggested that advice on safer sex is being ignored. A MORI poll for the Terence Higgins Trust in 1999 suggested that 56% of adults have not taken the disease into account before having casual sex. A campaign was launched by the Government at the end of 1998 to persuade mothers-to-be to have an HIV test. The prevalence of HIV among women giving birth in London has quadrupled since 1990 and only 30% of women who are HIV positive know that they are HIV positive (Murray, 1998).

A cure or vaccine has still not been discovered for acquired immunodeficiency syndrome (AIDS) even though recent drug combinations have slowed the rate of the progress of the disease within the individual. It still remains one of the major scourges among the infectious diseases in the UK.

Laws relating to AIDS and HIV

This country has never passed an AIDS/HIV Discrimination Act. Therefore, although those infected may be subject to venereal disease legislation or specific notification provisions, there are no specific laws protecting the confidentiality of sufferers, or preventing discrimination in the workplace. Those who come within the definition of disabled for the purposes of the Disability Discrimination Act 1995 may have the protection of that Act and the regulations made under it. In general, however, AIDS/HIV victims have only the basic laws, including the rights under the European Convention on Human Rights, which apply to everyone to protect them against unwarranted disclosure or unjustified discrimination.

There have been criminal convictions where an infected person has attempted to infect others. In Louisiana, USA, it was reported that a doctor who gave his lover the AIDS virus by injecting her with infected blood was given the maximum penalty of 50 years hard labour for attempted second-degree murder (*The Times*, 1999). In Missouri, a laboratory technician was convicted of stealing an HIV-tainted specimen and injecting it into his infant son to avoid paying child support (Bone, 1998). In the UK a man has been prosecuted for passing on to his girlfriend the HIV virus. Stephen Kelly was convicted of knowingly infecting a lover with HIV and was jailed for five years (Harris, 2001). He was prosecuted under the Scottish common law. It was announced by the Home Secretary that a new criminal offence of deliberately infecting a person with the HIV virus was to be created in England and Wales.

A nurse with AIDS and HIV

The UKCC issued guidelines relating to the duty of any registered practitioners who find that they are suffering from AIDS/HIV to report the situation to their employer. The NMC (2008) updated its guidance on blood-borne viruses in its A–Z advice sheet. It advised that:

> Nurses and midwives infected with a blood-borne virus should have their viral load monitored regularly and should not return to work unless agreed as fit to resume by a responsible medical officer, general practitioner or their occupational health consultant. The agreed viral load varies depending on the infection. Nurses and midwives should confirm with their own Occupational Health Department what is acceptable for their particular place of employment.

The guidance emphasises the importance of respecting the confidentiality of employees' health status.

Registrants who fail to comply with advice and guidance from the NMC could be subject to fitness to practice proceedings. It does not follow, however, that nurses would automatically lose their jobs. Clearly, if there were a greater risk to patients as a result of the situation, employers would have to find the nurse alternative suitable work.

Other health practitioners

Other registration bodies, such as the General Medical Council and the General Dental Council, also recognise the necessity of an infected practitioner notifying the relevant officer at work, and ensuring patient safety.

Failure to notify

What happens when a healthcare professional appears to disobey the guidance of his/her professional registration body? Can anyone else take it upon him/herself to report that information?

A reported case

In the case of *X* v. *Y* [1988] the court ordered an injunction to be issued to prevent the disclosure by the press of the identity of doctors suffering from AIDS. The facts are shown in Box 6.2.

Box 6.2 X v. Y [1988]

Two general practitioners were diagnosed as having contracted AIDS. They received counselling in a local hospital, continuing with their medical practice. A journalist heard of the situation from an employee of the health authority and wrote an article for a national newspaper. The health authority sought an injunction to prevent any further disclosure of the information obtained from patients' records.

The judge granted the injunction on the grounds that the records of hospital patients, particularly those suffering from this appalling condition, should be as confidential as the courts can properly make them. He rejected the defendant's argument that it was in the public interest for the public to know the identity of these doctors.

The judge did not, however, agree to the health authority's application for the name of the employee who had disclosed the information to the journalist. The Contempt of Court Act 1981 enabled journalists to keep their sources of information secret subject to specified exceptions and the judge held that these exceptions did not apply in this situation. The journalist was therefore entitled to protect his source.

The outcome of the case was that the doctors obtained the injunction preventing newspapers publishing their names, but the hospital did not obtain an order for the name of the informant employee to be released by the journalists, even though that employee was guilty of a disciplinary offence and could have faced dismissal if he or she had been identified.

Justification for disclosure of AIDS and HIV status

Sims (1997) discussed the duty of confidentiality in relation to the question of whether a physiotherapist needs to know if a patient has HIV. Sims concludes that except when progression to AIDS has occurred (in which case the diagnosis will be known to the therapist), a physiotherapist does not need to know a patient's HIV status. The reasons he gives are:

- A patient's HIV status does not determine the choice or effectiveness of therapy.
- The adoption of universal precautions provides optimum protection against transmission of HIV and does not depend upon a knowledge of who is, or is not, seropositive.
- Nor could it be argued that the patient should know of the therapist's status since the chance of contracting HIV from an infected physiotherapist is so remote as to represent virtually no risk.

Department of Health guidance

In 2005 the Department of Health updated its guidance on the management of health professionals with HIV/AIDS and notification to the patient (DH, 2005). It emphasised that

> Every effort should be made to avoid disclosure of the infected worker's identity, or information which would allow deductive disclosure. This should include the use of a media injunction as necessary to prevent disclosure of a health care worker's identity

It recommends that as far as is practicable, patients should only be notified if they have been at distinct risk of bleed-back from the particular exposure prone procedures performed on them by an HIV infected health care worker. Such patients should be contacted and encouraged to have pre-test discussion and HIV antibody testing. The guidance also covers dealing with the media. The Chief Medical Officer of Health's expert advisory group published guidance in 2008 (DH, 2008).

GMC guidance

The GMC has published supplementary guidance to its Confidentiality guidance on Disclosing Information on serious communicable diseases. It points out that

> The NHS (Venereal Diseases) Regulations 1974, The NHS Trusts (Venereal Diseases) Directions 1991 and The NHS Trusts and Primary Care Trusts (Sexually Transmitted Diseases) Directions 2000 state that various NHS bodies in England and Wales must 'take all necessary steps to secure that any information capable of identifying an individual... with respect to persons examined or treated for any sexually transmitted disease shall not be disclosed except – (a) for the purpose of communicating that information to a medical practitioner, or to a person employed under the direction of a medical practitioner in connection with the treatment of persons suffering from such disease or the prevention of the spread thereof, and (b) for the purpose of such treatment and prevention'. There are different interpretations of the Regulations and Directions, and concerns about their compatibility with the European Convention on Human Rights. In particular, there have

been concerns that a strict interpretation would prevent the disclosure of relevant information, except to other doctors or those working under their supervision, even with the patient's consent or to known sexual contacts in the public interest. Our view is that the Regulations and Directions do not preclude disclosure if it would otherwise be lawful at common law, for example with the patient's consent or in the public interest without consent.

Answering the question raised

In the case scenario Staff Nurse Grey should not have informed the press of the situation. She should have attempted to persuade her colleague to be open and honest with the employers by disclosing the situation to them. If the doctor failed to do this, then in a serious case, where danger to other colleagues and patients was feared, she could have notified the employers in writing of her concerns. However, she acted wrongly in going to the press.

Conclusions

The general principles which apply are: all registered practitioners have a professional duty to notify their employer of their AIDS/HIV status. Registered practitioners also have a duty to ensure that appropriate action is taken to ensure that patients are safe. This latter duty may require the disclosure of certain information to senior management or the appropriate person within the organisation. Any such disclosure should be made in complete confidence and be limited to the proper person.

References

Bone, J. (1998) Man injected his son with HIV to avoid payments. *The Times*, 7 December.

Department of Health (2005) HIV infected health care workers: guidance on the management of infected health care workers and patient notification. DH, London (1999, updated July 2005).

Department of Health (2008) *HIV Post-exposure Prophylaxis: Guidance from the UK Chief Medical Officers' Expert Advisory Group on AIDS*. DH, London.

Harris, G. (2001) Five years for the reckless lover who passed on HIV. *The Times*, 17 March.

Murray, I. (1998) Mothers-to-be are urged to have HIV test. *The Times*, 1 December.

Nursing and Midwifery Council (2006) *A–Z Advice Sheet: Blood-borne Viruses*. Last updated March 2006.

Sims, J. (1997) Confidentiality and HIV status. *Physiotherapy*, **83**(2), 90–6.

The Times (1999) AIDS attacker jailed. *The Times*, 19 February.

X v. *Y* [1988] 2 All ER 648.

CHAPTER 7

Human fertilisation and embryology issues

Box 7.1 Case scenario

A woman who was having *in vitro* fertilisation (IVF) treatment was involved in a road accident. Her sister, a nurse, who was with her at the time, knew that she was taking as part of the IVF treatment and passed this information on to those caring for her in the accident and emergency department, who obtained from her IVF clinic details of the drugs that she was on. Subsequently, the patient complained that this information should not have been passed on. She did not want anyone else to know that she was receiving fertility treatment. What is the law?

Introduction

There are certain exceptional circumstances in which, although a general duty of confidentiality applies, the law reinforces it by specific statutory provision. One such example is human fertilisation and embryology. This chapter considers the law, the changes which have taken place and how it applies to practice (Lee and Morgan, 2001; Birk, 2009).

Human Fertilisation and Embryology Act 1990 (as amended by the 2008 Act)

Section 33 of the Human Fertilisation and Embryology Act 1990 (as amended by the Human Fertilisation and Embryology Act 2008) restricts the disclosure of information relating to the register of individuals receiving treatment, services and any other information (which is held in confidence) that is obtained by any member or employee of the Human Fertilisation and Embryology Authority (http://www.hfea.gov.uk/). Permitted disclosures include those shown in Table 7.1.

Table 7.1 Permitted disclosures under section 33 of the Human Fertilisation and Embryology Act 1990 (as amended by section 25 of the Human Fertilisation and Embryology Act 2008).

25 Restrictions on disclosure of information
For section 33 of the 1990 Act (restrictions on disclosure of information) substitute—

'33A Disclosure of information
(1) No person shall disclose any information falling within section 31(2) which the person obtained (whether before or after the coming into force of section 24 of the Human Fertilisation and Embryology Act 2008) in the person's capacity as—
  (a) a member or employee of the Authority,
  (b) any person exercising functions of the Authority by virtue of section 8B or 8C of this Act (including a person exercising such functions by virtue of either of those sections as a member of staff or as an employee),
  (c) any person engaged by the Authority to provide services to the Authority,
  (d) any person employed by, or engaged to provide services to, a person mentioned in paragraph (c),
  (e) a person to whom a licence applies,
  (f) a person to whom a third party agreement applies, or
  (g) a person to whom directions have been given.
(2) Subsection (1) does not apply where—
  (a) the disclosure is made to a person as a member or employee of the Authority or as a person exercising functions of the Authority as mentioned in subsection (1)(b),
  (b) the disclosure is made to or by a person falling within subsection (1)(c) for the purpose of the provision of services which that person is engaged to provide to the Authority,
  (c) the disclosure is made by a person mentioned in subsection (1)(d) for the purpose of enabling a person falling within subsection (1)(c) to provide services which that person is engaged to provide to the Authority,
  (d) the disclosure is made to a person to whom a licence applies for the purpose of that person's functions as such,

(e) the disclosure is made to a person to whom a third party agreement applies for the purpose of that person's functions under that agreement,

(f) the disclosure is made in pursuance of directions given by virtue of section 24,

(g) the disclosure is made so that no individual can be identified from the information,

(h) the disclosure is of information other than identifying donor information and is made with the consent required by section 33B,

(i) the disclosure–
  (i) is made by a person who is satisfied that it is necessary to make the disclosure to avert an imminent danger to the health of an individual ('P'),
  (ii) is of information falling within section 31(2)(a) which could be disclosed by virtue of paragraph (h) with P's consent or could be disclosed to P by virtue of subsection (5), and
  (iii) is made in circumstances where it is not reasonably practicable to obtain P's consent,

(j) the disclosure is of information which has been lawfully made available to the public before the disclosure is made,

(k) the disclosure is made in accordance with sections 31ZA to 31ZE,

(l) the disclosure is required or authorised to be made–
  (i) under regulations made under section 33D, or
  (ii) in relation to any time before the coming into force of the first regulations under that section, under regulations made under section 251 of the National Health Service Act 2006,

(m) the disclosure is made by a person acting in the capacity mentioned in subsection (1)(a) or (b) for the purpose of carrying out the Authority's duties under section 8A,

(n) the disclosure is made by a person acting in the capacity mentioned in subsection (1)(a) or (b) in pursuance of an order of a court under section 34 or 35,

(o) the disclosure is made by a person acting in the capacity mentioned in subsection (1)(a) or (b) to the Registrar General in pursuance of a request under section 32,

(p) the disclosure is made by a person acting in the capacity mentioned in subsection (1)(a) or (b) to any body or person discharging a regulatory function for the purpose of assisting that body or person to carry out that function,

(q) the disclosure is made for the purpose of establishing in any proceedings relating to an application for an order under subsection (1) of section 54 of the Human Fertilisation and Embryology Act 2008 whether the condition specified in paragraph (a) or (b) of that subsection is met,

(r) the disclosure is made under section 3 of the Access to Health Records Act 1990,

(s) the disclosure is made under Article 5 of the Access to Health Records (Northern Ireland) Order 1993, or

(t) the disclosure is made necessarily for–

   (i) the purpose of the investigation of any offence (or suspected offence), or

   (ii) any purpose preliminary to proceedings, or for the purposes of, or in connection with, any proceedings.

(3) Subsection (1) does not apply to the disclosure of information in so far as–

   (a) the information identifies a person who, but for sections 27 to 29 of this Act or sections 33 to 47 of the Human Fertilisation and Embryology Act 2008, would or might be a parent of a person who instituted proceedings under section 1A of the Congenital Disabilities (Civil Liability) Act 1976, and

   (b) the disclosure is made for the purpose of defending such proceedings, or instituting connected proceedings for compensation against that parent.

(4) Paragraph (t) of subsection (2), so far as relating to disclosure for the purpose of the investigation of an offence or suspected offence, or for any purpose preliminary to, or in connection with proceedings, does not apply–

   (a) to disclosure of identifying donor information, or

   (b) to disclosure, in circumstances in which subsection (1) of section 34 of this Act applies, of information relevant to the determination of the question mentioned in that subsection, made by any person acting in a capacity mentioned in any of paragraphs (c) to (g) of subsection (1).

(5) Subsection (1) does not apply to the disclosure to any individual of information which–

   (a) falls within subsection (2) of section 31 of this Act by virtue of any of paragraphs (a) to (e) of that subsection, and

   (b) relates only to that individual or, in the case of an individual who is treated together with, or gives a notice under section 37 or 44 of the Human Fertilisation and Embryology Act 2008 in respect of, another, only to that individual and that other.

(6) In subsection (2)–

   (a) in paragraph (p) 'regulatory function' has the same meaning as in section 32 of the Legislative and Regulatory Reform Act 2006, and

(b) in paragraph (t) references to 'proceedings' include any formal procedure for dealing with a complaint.

(7) In this section 'identifying donor information' means information enabling a person to be identified as a person whose gametes were used in accordance with consent given under paragraph 5 of Schedule 3 for the purposes of treatment services or non-medical fertility services in consequence of which an identifiable individual was, or may have been, born.

33B Consent required to authorise certain disclosures

(1) This section has effect for the purposes of section 33A(2)(h).

(2) Subject to subsection (5), the consent required by this section is the consent of each individual who can be identified from the information.

(3) Consent in respect of a person who has not attained the age of 18 years ('C') may be given–
   (a) by C, in a case where C is competent to deal with the issue of consent, or
   (b) by a person having parental responsibility for C, in any other case.

(4) Consent to disclosure given at the request of another shall be disregarded unless, before it is given, the person requesting it takes reasonable steps to explain to the individual from whom it is requested the implications of compliance with the request.

(5) In the case of information which shows that any identifiable individual ('A') was, or may have been, born in consequence of treatment services, the consent required by this section does not include A's consent if the disclosure is necessarily incidental to the disclosure of information falling within section 31(2)(a).

(6) The reference in subsection (3) to parental responsibility is–
   (a) in relation to England and Wales, to be read in accordance with the Children Act 1989;
   (b) in relation to Northern Ireland, to be read in accordance with the Children (Northern Ireland) Order 1995;
   (c) in relation to Scotland, to be read as a reference to parental responsibilities and parental rights within the meaning of the Children (Scotland) Act 1995.

33C Power to provide for additional exceptions from section 33A(1)

(1) Regulations may provide for additional exceptions from section 33A(1).

(2) No exception may be made under this section for–
   (a) disclosure of a kind mentioned in paragraph (a) or (b) of subsection (4) of section 33A, or
   (b) disclosure in circumstances in which section 32 of this Act applies of information having the tendency mentioned in subsection (2) of that section, made by any person acting in a capacity mentioned in any of paragraphs (c) to (g) of subsection (1) of section 33A.

33D Disclosure for the purposes of medical or other research

(1) Regulations may–

    (a) make such provision for and in connection with requiring or regulating the processing of protected information for the purposes of medical research as the Secretary of State considers is necessary or expedient in the public interest or in the interests of improving patient care, and

    (b) make such provision for and in connection with requiring or regulating the processing of protected information for the purposes of any other research as the Secretary of State considers is necessary or expedient in the public interest.

(2) Regulations under subsection (1) may, in particular, make provision–

    (a) for requiring or authorising the disclosure or other processing of protected information to or by persons of any prescribed description subject to compliance with any prescribed conditions (including conditions requiring prescribed undertakings to be obtained from such persons as to the processing of such information),

    (b) for securing that, where prescribed protected information is processed by a person in accordance with the regulations, anything done by that person in so processing the information must be taken to be lawfully done despite any obligation of confidence owed by the person in respect of it,

    (c) for requiring fees of a prescribed amount to be paid to the Authority in prescribed circumstances by persons in relation to the disclosure to those persons of protected information under those regulations,

    (d) for the establishment of one or more bodies to exercise prescribed functions in relation to the processing of protected information under those regulations,

    (e) as to the membership and proceedings of any such body, and

    (f) as to the payment of remuneration and allowances to any member of any such body and the reimbursement of expenses.

(3) Where regulations under subsection (1) require or regulate the processing of protected information for the purposes of medical research, such regulations may enable any approval given under regulations made under section 251 of the National Health Service Act 2006 (control of patient information) to have effect for the purposes of the regulations under subsection (1) in their application to England and Wales.

(4) Subsections (1) to (3) are subject to subsections (5) to (8).

(5) Regulations under subsection (1) may not make any provision requiring or authorising the disclosure or other processing, for any purpose, of protected information, where that information is information from which an individual may be identified, if it would be reasonably practicable to

achieve that purpose otherwise than pursuant to such regulations, having regard to the cost of and technology available for achieving that purpose.

(6) Regulations under this section may not make provision for or in connection with the processing of protected information in a manner inconsistent with any provision made by or under the Data Protection Act 1998.

(7) Subsection (6) does not affect the operation of provisions made under subsection (2)(b).

(8) Before making any regulations under this section the Secretary of State shall consult such bodies appearing to the Secretary of State to represent the interests of those likely to be affected by the regulations as the Secretary of State considers appropriate.

(9) In this section–
'prescribed' means prescribed by regulations made by virtue of this section,
'processing', in relation to information, means the use, disclosure, or obtaining of the information or the doing of such other things in relation to it as may be prescribed for the purposes of this definition, and
'protected information' means information falling within section 31(2).'

Further exceptions to disclosure include where a person wishes to defend an action or institute compensation proceedings brought under the Congenital Disabilities (Civil Liability) Act 1976. Section 34 of the 1990 Act (as amended by the 2008 Act) permits disclosure in the interests of justice (Box 7.2).

Box 7.2 Section 34 of the Human Fertilisation and Embryology Act 1990, as amended by the 2008 Act: disclosure in the interests of justice

Where in any proceedings before a court the question whether a person is or is not the parent of a child by virtue of section 27 to 29 of this Act or sections 33 to 47 of the Human Fertilisation and Embryology Act 2008 falls to be determined, the court may on the application of any party to the proceedings make an order requiring the Human Fertilisation and Embryology Authority to disclose information. This information is specified in section 34(2).

In determining whether the interests of justice apply the court takes into account any representations of a person who may be affected by the disclosure, e.g. the welfare of the child, if under 18 years, and of any person under that age who may be affected by the disclosure. In civil cases the court can direct that the proceedings are held in camera (i.e. in secret).

Offences

Section 41 of the 1990 Act (as amended by the 2008 Act) makes it a criminal offence for any person to make a disclosure contrary to section 33 of the Act. The consent of the Director of Public Prosecution is required before criminal proceedings can be brought.

Disclosure with the consent of the person involved in the treatment

A permitted grounds for disclosure under section 33(4)(b) of the 1990 Act was where there was consent by the person or persons whose confidence would otherwise be protected. Consent had to be given for specific purposes for disclosure to a specific person. Following the implementation of the 1990 Act, this was found to be too restrictive an exception to the duty of confidentiality. It would not, for example, have covered the disclosure by the clinic in the situation shown in the case scenario in Box 7.1.

The law was therefore amended by the Human Fertilisation and Embryology (Disclosure of Information) Act 1992 to widen the consent provisions and facilitate disclosure in exceptional circumstances. The amendments introduced by the 1992 Act were subsequently incorporated into the 2008 Act and the 1992 Act was repealed. The revised provisions are shown in Table 7.1.

As a consequence of these provisions:

- The patient can give consent to disclosure to a specified person and to give general consent to disclosure within a wider circle of people where disclosure is necessary in connection with medical treatment, clinical audit or accounts audit;
- Before consent is given, reasonable steps must be taken to explain the implications of giving consent to the patient;
- Disclosure of information is also permissible in an emergency where the person disclosing is satisfied that the disclosure is necessary to avert imminent danger to the health of the patient and at the time it is not reasonably practicable to obtain the patient's consent;

- The clinician can also disclose information to his legal adviser where necessary for the purposes preliminary to or in connection with legal proceedings;
- Access to records of treatment can be given to personal representatives and those acting on behalf of the incapacitated patient in litigation.

Power is given for regulations permitting other disclosures and also for medical or other research to be drawn up.

The significance of the changes to the 1990 Act can be seen from the facts in the situation shown in the Case scenario box. Under the 1990 Act the woman injured in the road accident would have had a right of action in respect of the disclosure. However, under the 1992 Act, now incorporated in the 2008 Act, if it can be shown that it was an emergency situation to prevent danger to the patient and it was not practicable to obtain her consent, then disclosure can be made.

Children born as a result of treatment under the Act

There is a right of access to information for those who have been born as a result of treatment under the Act. Section 31 as replaced by the 2008 Act requires the authority to keep a register of information. Section 31ZA enables a person over 16 years to request information as to genetic parentage etc. Section 31ZB enables a request to be made for information as to intended spouse etc. Section 31ZC gives the Authority power to inform donor of request for information; Section 31ZD covers the provision to donor of information about resulting children; Section 31ZE covers the provision of information about donor-conceived genetic siblings; Section 31ZF gives the Authority power of Authority to keep a voluntary contact register and Section 31ZG covers financial assistance for a person setting up or keeping a voluntary contact register. These sections can be viewed on the Office of Public Sector Information website (http:// www.opsi.gov. uk/).

An application to the Human Fertilisation and Embryology Authority under section 31 will result in information which shows that the individual has been born as a result of treatment services being made available. The Authority must comply with a request under subsection (2) if:

(a) the information contained in the register shows that the applicant is a relevant individual, and

(b) the applicant has been given a suitable opportunity to receive proper counselling about the implications of compliance with the request.

The wording is interesting: the applicant does not have to have the counselling, merely the opportunity for it to be given.

Where a request is made by a person under 18 years, the Regulations cannot require the Authority to give the applicant any information which identifies the donor.

Section 31(4) enables disclosure of information contained on the register to be made which shows that a person other than a parent of the applicant would or might be a parent of the applicant. However, there is express provision that the regulations cannot require the Human Fertilisation and Embryology Authority to give any information as to the identity of a person whose gametes have been used or from whom an embryo has been taken. The applicant can require the Authority to state whether the applicant, and a person specified in the request as a person whom the applicant proposes to marry or with whom the applicant proposes to enter into a civil partnership, or with whom the applicant is in an intimate physical relationship or with whom the applicant proposes to enter into an intimate physical relationship would or might be related.

Those under 16 years

Those under 16 years do not have the right to ascertain if he or she and an intended spouse or civil partner are related and the Authority is expressly forbidden to comply with the request for information (S31ZB(5)).

Conclusions

The Human Fertilisation and Embryology Act 1990 as amended by the 2008 Act traces a careful path between preserving the confidentiality rights of those who have been in receipt of treatment services and the interests of children born from those services. The Human Fertilisation and Embryology Authority has prepared and regularly revised a code of practice to guide treatment centres in the implementation of the legislation and practice not covered by specific legislative provisions. Further information can be obtained from the HFEA website (http://www.hfea.gov.uk/).

References

Birk, D. (2009) *Human Fertilisation and Embryology: The New Law*. Jordans New Law Series, London.

Lee, R. G. and Morgan, D. (2001) *Human Fertilisation and Embryology Act 1990*. Blackstone Press, London.

CHAPTER 8

The Department of Health, NHS trusts and patient confidentiality

> ## Box 8.1 Case scenario
>
> Nurse Salmon worked in the gynaecology ward at a hospital and was known to gossip about her patients over lunch with colleagues. She did not usually mention their names. However, on one occasion a well known television star was admitted to have a termination, and in confidence Nurse Salmon told her friends about this, mentioning the person by name. If this comes to the notice of her employers, what action, if any, should they take?

Introduction

In Chapter 1 the various sources of the duty of confidentiality were identified and it was noted that one of the sources was an implied term in the contract of employment. This term would require every employee who comes across confidential information in the course of employment to respect that confidentiality. Failure to do so could result in disciplinary proceedings, the ultimate sanction of which is dismissal. As an implied term, the employee may never have explicitly agreed to that term being included in the contract, but by operation of law, when a contract of employment comes into being the law would expect that certain terms would be implied in order to make business sense of that contract.

Such a term would be implied into the contract of every employee, not just those who, as registered practitioners, come under a professional code of conduct. Each employer, therefore, has a responsibility to enforce the duty of confidentiality across the organisation. Clear policies should be in existence for confidentiality to be respected. Sometimes employers might require an express term of confidentiality to be included in each contract of employment and registered practitioners might have an express duty to obey the professional standards of their registration body written into their employment contracts. Oral warnings, written warnings and, ultimately, dismissal should follow breaches of the duty of confidentiality.

In practice, however, as many nurses would agree, hospitals, community health departments and GP surgeries are rife with gossip about patient information. The situation set out in the case scenario is probably not atypical in that sensational information would rapidly spread across an organisation.

Nurses and other staff pass confidential information to colleagues when the justification for those colleagues having that information (i.e. it is in the best interests of the care of the patient) is not present. Regretfully it would probably be agreed that hospital staff are not in general good guardians of patient confidentiality.

Caldicott Committee

Concern about the need to improve the way in which the NHS managed patient confidentiality led to the appointment of a committee chaired by Dame Fiona Caldicott. It reported in December 1997. Included in its recommendations was the need to raise awareness of confidentiality requirements. It specifically recommended the establishment of a network of Caldicott 'guardians' of patient information throughout the NHS. Subsequently, a steering group was set up to oversee the implementation of the report's recommendations.

Following a consultation period the NHS Executive (NHSE) issued a circular on the establishment of Caldicott guardians (NHSE, 1999). The circular gives advice on the appointment of the guardians, the programme of work for the first year for improving the way each organisation handles confidential patient information and identifies the resources, training and other support for the guardians.

The guardian

Each health authority, special health authority, NHS trust and primary care group was required to appoint a Caldicott guardian no later than 31 March

Table 8.1 Action to be taken to support the guardian.

- Develop local protocols governing the disclosure of patient information to other organisations
- Restrict access to patient information within each organisation by enforcing strict need-to-know principles
- Regularly review and justify the uses of patient information
- Improve organisational performance across a range of related areas: database design, staff induction, training, compliance with guidance, etc.

1999. Ideally, the guardian should be at board level, be a senior health professional and have responsibility for promoting clinical governance within the organisation. The name and address of the guardian is to be notified to the NHSE. Action to be undertaken by each NHS organisation in support of the guardian is shown in Table 8.1. The guardian is expected to liaise closely with others involved in patient information, such as information, management and technology security officers and data protection officers.

In making the appointment and defining the role of the guardian, the duties which are not to be delegated should be clarified. Guardians are responsible for agreeing and reviewing internal protocols governing the protection and use of patient-identifiable information by the staff of their organisation and must be satisfied that these proposals address the requirements for national guidance/policy and law. The operation of these policies must also be monitored. Policies for inter-agency disclosure of patient information must also be agreed and reviewed, to facilitate cross-boundary working.

Resources/training/action

The preservation of the confidentiality of patient information is seen as a cornerstone of the NHS information strategy. Therefore, the NHSE advised that the modernisation funds which were made available to support local implementation of the information strategy could be used to support Caldicott guardians. Seminars have been and are being organised within each region of the NHS and persons interested are advised to make contact with the NHSE. The NHS circular outlined the action which each organisation was required to take in the first year. The main activities are shown in Table 8.2.

Table 8.2 Specific tasks of Caldicott guardians in the first year.

- A management audit of existing procedures for protection and using patient-identifiable information leading to a report for the guardian to present to the senior management team as a 'stock-take'
- The development of an improvement plan that will address any identified deficiencies

Confidentiality and electronic records

A major concern about the implementation of a national system of electronic patient records is that of confidentiality. The Department of Health, the General Medical Council and the Office of the Information Commissioner issued joint guidance on the use of IT equipment and access to patient data on 25 April 2007. It can be down loaded from the relevant websites. The joint statement was made to ensure that all those who have access to patient information in the course of their work are clear about what is expected of them. The DH strongly supported the call of the ICO for stronger penalties to apply where individuals obtain information unlawfully, and for the law to be changed to provide the possibility of a custodial sentence for those found guilty. In the case of the new NHS IM&T systems, authorised individuals will have to sign a statement to indicate their understanding and agreement to adhere to the standards set out in the joint guidance.

The Information Commissioner published his views on NHS electronic care records in January 2007 in response to the concerns of those made to the ICO that their health records would be available to everyone across the NHS. The ICO had been informed by NHS Connecting for Health that every one, in the initial trial areas, whose Summary Care Record (current medication, known allergies and adverse reactions) are to be loaded onto the NHS Care Record Service will be contacted and given information about their options. Once the information is uploaded, patients can choose to remove some or even all of the information initially loaded or keep the uploaded information but make the Summary Care Record invisible. The ICO also referred to the range of access controls to be introduced by the NHS as the new systems develop. All access to the Summary Care Record will be logged and unusual access will be investigated by the Caldicott guardian (see above). NHS Connecting for Health had also informed the ICO that health information uploaded onto the NHS Care Records Service will not be accessible to any other organisations beyond the NHS without the patient's explicit consent, except where this is allowed or required by law. The ICO stated that the NHS must continue to comply with the Data Protection Act 1998 and this is vital to guarantee that public confidence is maintained. The ICO would monitor the implementation and operation of the NHS Care Records Service to ensure that patients are provided with adequate information and choices and that their health data is maintained in a safe and secure way.

The National Audit Office in its progress report published on 15 May 2008 (NAO, 2008) on the national programme for electronic medical records stated that the Care Records Service is unlikely to be in place before 2014–15 at the earliest, because of serious delays in installing new software. It made several recommendations, including the fact that the DH and NHS should give priority to data protection; monitor levels of public confidence; and review how the levels are being influenced by its communications about the protections in place to secure and manage access to care records. The role of the NIGB in relation to the NHS Care Records Guarantee is considered in Chapter 3.

Answering the question posed in the case scenario

One of the results of the implementation of the Caldicott recommendations and the establishment of guardians should be that the culture of confidentiality and sensitivity in handling patient information within NHS organisations should improve. Staff should appreciate that to disclose patient-identifiable information in unjustified circumstances is a serious disciplinary offence for which action will be taken by the employers. Nurse Salmon is clearly in breach of the implied term in her contract of employment, as well as being guilty of professional misconduct. She should face disciplinary proceedings and should also be reported to the NMC.

Guardians should aim to raise awareness of the need to protect confidentiality across the organisation so that each individual member of staff understands the seriousness of any breach of confidentiality. Disciplinary action is a sign to each individual member of staff (including doctors) that the duty of confidentiality is taken extremely seriously by the organisation. It is important, however, to remember that Caldicott guardians are only part of the programme to improve the way in which the NHS uses patient information.

The National Information Governance Board for Health and Social Care

Section 61 of the Health and Social Care Act 2001 provided for the establishment of a Patient Information Advisory Group. Regulations were drawn up by the Secretary of State to make provision for:

- the persons or bodies who are to be represented by members of the Advisory Group,
- the terms of appointment of members,
- the proceedings of the Advisory Group, and
- the payment by the Secretary of State of such expenses and allowances as he may determine.

Prior to the regulations under Section 60 (see Chapter 3) being placed before parliament, the Secretary of State was obliged to consult with the Advisory Group. In 2009 the Patient Information Advisory Group was replaced by the National Information and Governance Board for Health and Social Care (http://www.nigb.nhs.uk/). The Board was established under section 157 of the Health and Social Care Act 2008. The NIGB website hosts the NHS Care Record Guarantee (http://www.nigb.nhs.uk/guarantee/; see below). Its overall role is to support improvements to information governance practice in health and social care.

The functions of the new Board include:

- to monitor the practice followed by relevant bodies in relation to the processing of relevant information
- to keep the Secretary of State, and such bodies as the Secretary of State may designate by direction, informed about the practice being followed by relevant bodies in relation to the processing of relevant information
- to publish guidance on the practice to be followed in relation to the processing of relevant information
- to advise the Secretary of State on particular matters relating to the processing of relevant information by any person and
- to advise persons who process relevant information on such matters relating to the processing of relevant information by them as the Secretary of State may from time to time designate by direction

The Board must, in exercising its functions, seek to improve the practice followed by relevant bodies in relation to the processing of relevant information.

'Relevant information' is defined as:
- patient information
- any other information obtained or generated in the course of the provision of the health service and
- any information obtained or generated in the course of the exercise by a local social services authority in England of its adult social services functions.

'Patient information' means:

- information (however recorded) which relates to the physical or mental health or condition of an individual ('P'), to the diagnosis of P's condition or to P's care or treatment, and
- information (however recorded) which is to any extent derived directly or indirectly, from that information whether or not the identity of the individual in question is ascertainable from the information.

See Chapter 3 for the work of the Ethics and Confidentiality Committee (ECC) which undertakes the responsibilities of the National Information Governance Board under section 251 of the NHS Act 2006 in considering and advising on ethical issues relating to the processing of health or social care information as referred to it by the NIGB.

Conclusions

It is impossible to overemphasise the importance of the Department of Health and every NHS organisation in creating a culture of confidentiality within each department. Only if employers take breaches of confidentiality seriously and use disciplinary action to enforce the duty of confidentiality can patients begin to feel that their confidential information is respected. Sometimes staff are concerned about safety and resource issues within an organisation and are faced with an apparent conflict between the need to make known serious deficiencies (i.e. whistle blowing) and the duty of confidentiality. It is to this apparent conflict which we look in the next chapter.

References

National Audit Office (2008) *The National Programme for IT in the NHS – Progress Since 2006*. HC 484-1 Session 2007-8, Stationery Office, London.

NHS Executive (1999) *Caldicott Guardians*. Health Service Circular 1999/012, 31 January. NHSE, Department of Health, London.

CHAPTER 9

The law relating to whistle blowing

Box 9.1 Case scenario

Alex Black, a staff nurse on an intensive care unit, was extremely concerned about the lack of adequate staffing levels on the unit. He had put his concerns in writing to his manager, but no action appeared to have been taken. On one weekend there was such a lack of staff that it was impossible to ensure that one nurse was attending every patient on a ventilator at all times. A young girl, injured in a road accident, was brought into the unit following surgery, and was placed on a ventilator. Alex was asked to monitor her care as well as that of another patient being ventilated. The girl died and Alex considered that this might not have happened if there had been adequate staff levels. He knows that the family is ignorant of how low the standards of care were and is anxious that they should be notified. Would it be lawful for him to tell them?

Introduction

In the previous chapter the role of the Caldicott guardians was discussed, together with the responsibility that each NHS organisation has to establish protocols for the protection of the confidentiality of patient-identifiable information. It is important, however, to ensure that the duty of confidentiality is not used to stifle the raising of legitimate concerns about the functioning of the organisation and that staff have the opportunity to bring these concerns to the attention of management. Trusts have sometimes required staff to sign up to 'gagging' clauses in their contracts which prevents them from notifying external persons about their concerns.

Professional duty of staff to raise concerns

Practitioners registered with the NMC have a professional responsibility to raise any concerns. In its code of conduct, the NMC (2008) requires registered practitioners to 'Manage risk', which is explained as:

- You must act without delay if you believe that you, a colleague or anyone else may be putting someone at risk
- You must inform someone in authority if you experience problems that prevent you working within this Code or other nationally agreed standards
- You must report your concerns in writing if problems in the environment of care are putting people at risk

As part of the duty to work with others to protect and promote the health and wellbeing of those in your care, their families and carers, and the wider community, the NMC states its registered practitioners must:

- work with colleagues to monitor the quality of your work and maintain the safety of those in your care.

The Health Professions Council

In its revised Code of Practice, the HPC (2008) stated that registrants were required to:

> ...protect service users if you believe that any situation puts them in danger. This includes the conduct, performance or health of a colleague. The safety of service users must come before any personal or professional loyalties at all times. As soon as you become aware of a situation that puts a service user in danger, you should discuss the matter with a senior colleague or another appropriate person.

The case of Margaret Haywood (see below), a nurse registered with the NMC, illustrates the problems of a nurse attempting to draw concerns to public notice and but at the same time attempting to recognise the duty of confidentiality.

Protection under legislation

The Public Interest Disclosure Act 1998 provides statutory protection against victimisation for any employee who raises legitimate concerns with the employer. Protected disclosures are defined in section 1 of the Act and cover the situations listed in Table 9.1. The Act extends the rights under the Employment Rights Act 1996 which gives protection to employees not to suffer any detriment from the employer in health and safety cases.

The protected disclosures in Table 9.1 are extensive and would cover most of the situations where a registered practitioner would have a professional duty to inform an appropriate person or authority under the Code of Professional Conduct of his or her registration body.

Table 9.1 Protected disclosures under the Public Interest Disclosure Act 1998.

- That a criminal offence has been, is being, or likely to be committed
- That a person has failed, is failing or is likely to fail to comply with any legal obligation to which he is subject
- That a miscarriage of justice has occurred, is occurring, or is likely to occur
- That the health or safety of any individual has been, is being, or is likely to be endangered
- That the environment has been, is being, or is likely to be damaged
- That information tending to show any matter falling within any of the above paragraphs has been, is being, or is likely to be deliberately concealed

How is the disclosure to be made?

Under the Act the disclosure is only protected if certain conditions are satisfied. The employee must have made the disclosure in good faith to his or her employer or other responsible person (S43C). Where the employee reasonably believes that a person other than the employer is to blame, then the disclosure can be made to that other person.

Disclosure is also protected if it is made in the course of obtaining legal advice (S43D) or, if the employer is a body whose members are appointed by a Minister of the Crown, the disclosure can be made to a Minister of the Crown

(S43E). This would cover disclosures by employees working within the NHS. The Secretary of State has the power to specify other persons to whom disclosures can be made (S43F). Disclosures to other persons (i.e .those not included above) are protected if the conditions set out in Table 9.2 and Table 9.3 are satisfied (S43G). The conditions referred to in Table 9.2 include the reasonable belief that the employee would be subjected to detriment by the employer if he or she makes the disclosure.

Table 9.2 Conditions for protected disclosures under S43G.

- The employee makes the disclosure in good faith
- He reasonably believes that the information disclosed, and any allegations contained in it, are substantially true
- He does not make the disclosure for personal gain
- Any of the conditions in subsection 2 is met (Table 9.3)
- In all the circumstances of the case, it is reasonable for him to make the disclosure (Table 9.4)

Table 9.3 Conditions required under S43G.

- That at the time he makes the disclosure the worker reasonably believes that he will be subjected to a detriment by his employer if he makes a disclosure to this employer or another person under S43F.
- That he reasonably believes that it is likely that evidence relating to the relevant failure will be concealed or destroyed if he makes the disclosure to his employer.
- That he has previously made a disclosure of substantially the same information to his employer or a person specified under S43F.
- Factors determining the reasonableness of the disclosure are listed in Table 9.4.

Table 9.4 Factors determining the reasonableness of disclosure under S43G.

- The identity of the person to whom it is made
- The seriousness of the failure
- Whether it is continuing or likely to occur in future
- Whether the disclosure is made in breach of a duty of confidentiality
- Previous disclosures to the employer or to another person prescribed by the Secretary of State
- Compliance with any procedure specified for making disclosures

Special provisions apply where there is a disclosure of an exceptionally serious failure (S43H). Such a disclosure is protected if the employee:

- makes the disclosure in good faith
- reasonably believing the allegations to be true
- is not making the disclosure for personal gain
- in all the circumstances it is reasonable to make the disclosure and
- it is reasonable to make it to that particular person

Gagging of an employee

The Act states that any provision in an agreement is void in so far as it purports to preclude an employee from making a protected disclosure. Thus, if a trust attempts to introduce a term in a contract of employment which prevents an employee making a disclosure which comes under the protection of the Act, that term is void.

Effect of the Act

The effect of the Act is that an employee who makes a disclosure defined as protected in the circumstances set out in the Act is protected from suffering any detriment. Any dismissal or action short of dismissal could be challenged by an application to an employment tribunal. Each NHS Trust is required to draw up policies and procedures to implement the Act (DH, 1999).

Procedures for bringing concerns to the attention of managers

Each NHS organisation should have established a procedure to ensure that it is possible for staff to alert senior management of failures within the organisation which could endanger health or safety or are of public concern. Any employee who has concerns which come within the provisions of Table 9.1 should follow the procedure to ensure that senior management attention is given to these disclosures. The Report of the Bristol Inquiry emphasised the importance of establishing an openness within NHS organisations so that respect and honesty with patients is part of the philosophy of the organisation. (Bristol Royal Infirmary, 2001). In addition, the concept of clinical governance and the statutory duty under section 18 of the Health Act 1999 should ensure that Trust Boards are sensitive to the need to address concerns raised by staff. The Care Quality Commission (replacing the Healthcare Commission) as watchdog of standards within the NHS also has a role to play in ensuring that staff concerns about standards in the NHS are investigated.

The case of Margaret Haywood

Concern was expressed about the striking off from the nursing and midwifery register of Margaret Haywood following her actions in reporting on TV abuses of elderly patients. The Council for Healthcare Regulatory Excellence (CHRE) issued a statement saying that it acknowledged public concern around the case, explaining its function but noting that it had no powers in relation to decisions which result in removal from the register. In these cases, the registrant has the right to appeal against such a decision.

The CHRE stated it had requested a copy of the transcript of this case from the NMC and would review it and would publish a report on the conduct and outcome of the case when all legal processes had been concluded. Subsequently the NMC and the Royal College of Nursing (RCN) made a joint statement:

> This was an extremely difficult and complex case in which the NMC panel had to balance Ms Haywood's duty to protect patient confidentiality with her duty to raise concerns about poor standards of care. The NMC and RCN put forward terms of settlement for the Court's consideration and the Court approved those terms which led to the replacement of the striking off order with a 12 month caution.

The NMC also announced that it had been working with key professional and patient groups to develop information that will support nurses and midwives to raise and escalate concerns they may have that people could be at risk of harm. The Council is to publish guidance on whistle blowing for consultation in January 2010.

The British Medical Association has set up a whistle blower helpline because of growing evidence of staff reluctance to speak out for fear of recrimination. The helpline is part of new guidelines (Lister, 2009). In 2008, to mark the 10th anniversary of the Act, the British Standards Institute published standards (BSI, 2008) for whistle blowing which can be down loaded free of charge from its website.

Case scenario

Alex should ensure that his concerns are raised at a senior level within the organisation. He should not at this stage pass his views on to the family of the dead patient. If he receives no appropriate response from senior management and considers that a 'cover up' is taking place, then he should be able to raise his concerns with higher levels of management, including the chief executive and the chairman of the trust. If they fail to respond appropriately, then there may be justification for bringing his concerns to the attention of the Secretary of State.

There would be no justification for informing the press before he had exhausted all avenues within the NHS. Those charged with the clinical governance of NHS services should ensure that there are appropriate procedures for staff to make known their legitimate concerns. Staff should ensure that they utilise these procedures, acting in good faith but at the same time, as far as it is possible, protecting patient confidentiality.

Conclusions

'Making Amends' (DH, 2003) a consultation by the Department of Health on a new scheme for clinical negligence compensation, recommended that there should be a duty of candour placed on healthcare professionals and managers to inform patients when they become aware of a possible negligent action or omission. This recommendation was not, however, included in the NHS Redress Act 2006 under which the new clinical negligence scheme is to be established. Whilst the Bristol Inquiry (Bristol Royal Infirmary, 2001) recommended an honest open culture in the NHS, there are still many factors which make it difficult for health professionals to raise concerns with senior management and ensure that action is taken. Despite the statutory provisions giving whistle blowers protection, there is still not a culture of openness and honesty within health and social care.

References

Bristol Royal Infirmary (2001) *Learning from Bristol: the Report of the Public Inquiry into Children's Heart Surgery at the Bristol Royal Infirmary 1984–1995*. Command Paper CM 5207 July 2001; http://www.bristol-inquiry.org.uk/.

British Standards Institute (2008) PAS (publicly available specification) 1998 *Whistle-blowing Arrangements Code of Practice*. BSI, London. Available from: http://www.bsigroup.com/en/sectorsandservices/Forms/PAS-19982008-Whistleblowing/.

Department of Health (1999) *Public Disclosure Act 1998: Whistleblowing in the NHS*. Health Service Circular (1999) HSC 1999/198. Department of Health, London.

Department of Health (2003) *Making Amends: a Consultation Paper Setting Out Proposals for Reforming the Approach to Clinical Negligence in the NHS*. DH, London.

Health Professions Council (2008) *Standards of Conduct, Performance and Ethics*. HPC, London.

Lister, S. (2009) Doctors set up whistleblower helpline as concerns grow for patient safety in NHS. *The Times*, 27 June.

Nursing and Midwifery Council (2008) *The Code: Standards of Conduct, Performance and Ethics for Nurses and Midwives*. NMC, London.

CHAPTER 10

Child care and the duty of confidentiality

Box 10.1 Case scenario

Jane told Angela White, a paediatric staff nurse, that she was being abused by her father, but did not want anyone to be told. Jane was 14 years old, intelligent and mature for her age. What is the law?

Introduction

The scenario above illustrates several conflicting legal principles.

The first is the duty of confidentiality in relation to information disclosed by a patient, which can apply, in certain circumstances, to information disclosed by children.

The second legal principle is the duty of care owed by the nurse to the child and the need to ensure that the child is protected.

The third legal principle is the public interest in securing the conviction of a criminal, since sexual relations with a girl under 16 years of age is a criminal offence.

Duty of confidentiality towards a child

In the Gillick case (*Gillick* v. *West Norfolk and Wisbech Area Health Authority* [1986]), the House of Lords established the principle that a mature child who understood the significance of a proposed treatment could give a valid consent. Such a child has become known as a 'Gillick competent child', the words now being gradually replaced by the phrase 'competent according to Lord Fraser's guidelines'. However, while a Gillick competent child can give consent to medical, surgical and dental treatment, and all associated diagnostic and anaesthetic procedures, a child (a person under 18 years) cannot refuse to give consent to life-saving treatment and the court would overrule any such refusal in the best interests of the child. The court overruled the refusal by a girl of 16 to have life-saving treatment. The girl was suffering from anorexia and refused to have treatment (*Re W (a minor) (Medical Treatment)*, 1992). More recently, the court ordered a 15-year-old girl to have a heart transplant (*Re M (Medical treatment: consent)* [1999]).

Similar principles apply in the duty of confidentiality to a child. If the child is 'Gillick competent' and confidentiality is in the best interests of the child, then the confidences of the child can be respected. Many paediatric nurses receive information from children which they do not pass on to the parents or guardians of the child.

Duty of care to the child

There would, however, be circumstances where the welfare of the child requires such confidences to be passed to the appropriate person. In the scenario here, Jane is said to be mature at 14 years of age, but she is the victim of abuse. Jane's interests and protection require that the appropriate child protection agencies are made aware of this abuse in order that she can be made safe from the abuser and receive counselling.

The Children Act 1989 sets out as a basic principle of law the fact that the 'welfare of the child is the paramount consideration'.

This is the test which Staff Nurse White must apply to the situation. Does Jane's welfare require that notification of the abuse is passed on? The answer must surely be yes. Obviously Staff Nurse White must make it clear to Jane that she cannot keep her confidences but must, for Jane's protection, ensure that the child protection agencies are notified. Staff Nurse White should also ensure that Jane obtains assistance and counselling. Even if the young person is over 16 years and has requested that the information be kept secret, there may be circumstances, particularly where a younger sibling is at risk, in reporting the abuse to the appropriate person.

The application of the principle that the 'welfare of the child is the paramount consideration' requires a balancing act. On one hand, the practitioner needs to take note of harm resulting from a suggested course of action; on the other hand, this needs to be assessed in the light of the benefits which arise. For example, a 15-year-old boy might disclose to a nurse that he stole from a shop. If this was an isolated incident the nurse might decide that it was not in the boy's best interests for the child protection agencies to be notified, thus respecting his confidence with suitable warnings against repetition. It is a question of judgment over what is the appropriate action, and junior staff would probably wish to seek advice from senior staff. In one sense this would be a breach of confidentiality, but it would be justified in the interests of the patient, since the nurse requires advice from a senior colleague on the appropriate action to take.

Child protection procedures

Professionals caring for children should be familiar with the local arrangements. They should know the procedure to be followed if abuse is suspected, the name of the reporting person, and what action to take.

The child healthcare practitioner should also be familiar with the child protection provisions of the Children Act 1989 and understand how an emergency protection order can be obtained and how it applies and the significance of a child assessment order (Gibson *et al.*, 2001). The topic of child protection and the checking of potential employees is considered in Chapter 15.

Duty to report a crime

There are very few specific circumstances in which the public has a duty to report a crime. Some of these were considered in the second chapter of this book. However, where harm to children is suspected and there is a likelihood of continuing offences against children, then the practitioner would have a duty to make this information known to the appropriate authority in the public interest. This is an exception to the duty of confidentiality and is recognised by most professional organisations. In particular, the NMC recognises the duty of an NMC practitioner to make such information known in the public interest:

> Under common law, staff are permitted to disclose personal information in order to prevent and support detection, investigation and punishment of serious crime and/or to prevent abuse or serious harm to others. Each case must be judged on its merits. Examples could include disclosing information in relation to crimes against the person e.g. rape, child abuse, murder, kidnapping, or as a result of injuries sustained from knife or gun shot wounds. These decisions are complex and must take

account of both the public interest in ensuring confidentiality against the public interest in disclosure. Disclosures should be proportionate and limited to relevant details (NMC, 2009).

Similarly, the HPC in the section on public interest in its guidance on confidentiality (HPC, 2008) recognises that there are occasions where confidential information must be disclosed in the public interest and states:

> You should still take appropriate steps to get the service user's consent (if possible) before you disclose the information. You should keep them informed about the situation as much as you can. However, this might not be possible or appropriate in some circumstances, such as when you disclose information to prevent or report a serious crime.

Record keeping

When healthcare professionals disclose confidential information, the importance of record keeping cannot be exaggerated. It is essential that the practitioner records the reasons why confidential information was passed on and what exactly was disclosed. If there is a subsequent allegation of breach of confidentiality, then that recorded information should provide a defence for the practitioner.

For example, if a nurse has a reasonable suspicion that injuries being shown by a child were the result of non-accidental injury, he or she should record the nature of the injuries, and any other evidence suggesting abuse, along with the action taken. Butler (1994) has suggested a simple chart incorporating descriptions of type and extent of injuries and grades of mood/pain which can be used as a paediatric assessment sheet.

Conclusion

The issues of professional judgment which arise in relation to the confidentiality of information received from children are exacting. Assistance to health visitors and nursing staff can be obtained from the Caldicott guardian, the person appointed within NHS trusts to set standards and monitor the respect for patient confidentiality (see Chapter 8). It is important for a practitioner caring for children to support their personal development and growth towards autonomy and, therefore, where reasonable, respect their confidences. However, this must be balanced against the need to secure their welfare and best interests. The topic of child protection and checking of employees is considered in Chapter 15.

References

Butler, K. (1994) Nurse-aid management of children 1: accidents. *British Journal of Nursing*, **3**(11), 579–82.

Gibson, C., Grice, J., James, R. and Mulholland, S. (2001) *The Children Act Explained.* The Stationery Office, London.

Gillick v. *West Norfolk and Wisbech Area Health Authority* [1986] 1AC112.

Health Professions Council (2008) *Confidentiality; Guidance for Registrants.* HPC, London.

Nursing and Midwifery Council (2009) *Advice Sheet: Confidentiality.* NMC, London.

Re M (Medical treatment: consent) [1999] 2 FLR 1097.

Re W (a minor) (Medical Treatment) [1992] 4 All ER 627.

Terminal illness and the duty of confidentiality

Box 11.1 Case scenario

David Jones returned from theatre where the surgeon had simply opened and closed him up with a diagnosis of inoperable cancer. His wife and daughter came to see him later and were informed of this by Staff Nurse Grey. They decided that David should not be told. What is the law?

Introduction

The situation outlined in the Box 11.1 is not unusual in health care, particularly in the care of elderly people and those suffering from terminal illness. Relatives are often informed before the patient, and they then ask health staff to keep this information from the patient because they believe that they are acting in the best interests of the patient, that the patient could not cope with the news, and that they will tell the patient when the 'time' comes. The 'time' is never clearly defined. Telling the relatives first is, of course, a reversal of what should be the legal situation.

The patient's right

The duty of confidentiality is owed to the patient. It is in theory the right of the patient to ask health professionals to keep information from the relatives. If the patient believes that he would prefer his wife and daughter not to know his diagnosis and prognosis, then that is his legal right, even if this makes communication between relatives and staff difficult. However, when information is first given to the relatives and not to the patient, the relatives acquire power over that information which the law does not give to them. Their refusal to allow a competent adult patient to obtain necessary information has no legal basis. Only if the patient lacks the requisite mental capacity to understand the information would health professionals be justified in giving the information to relatives acting in the best interests of the patient under the provisions of the Mental Capacity Act 2005 (see below).

European Convention on Human Rights

Article 8 of the European Convention on Human Rights recognises the right of respect for private and family life, home and correspondence. This right could be used as the basis of a legal action if a patient considered that there had been a breach of confidentiality. This is considered in Chapter 1 of this book.

Incompetent patients

There are only two exceptions to the principle that the patient should receive the information first: when the patient lacks the mental capacity to deal with that information; and when the information must be withheld because it would cause serious harm to the mental or physical health or condition of the patient.

A person with severe learning disabilities, or an elderly person suffering from Alzheimer's disease may not have the capacity to take in information and make decisions on their own account. In such cases, the Mental Capacity Act 2005 would apply. The staff would have to give information to the relatives. Relatives have the right under the Act to make decisions on behalf of a mentally incapacitated person. If an adult is incapable of making decisions for him- or herself about serious medical treatment, then the doctor must make the decision, in the best interests of the patient, taking into account the prognosis and what treatment should be given according to the reasonable standard of the profession in accordance with the steps set out in the Mental Capacity Act 2005. In the absence of relatives or friends who could be consulted about the patient's wishes, beliefs etc., an independent mental capacity advocate must be appointed who could inform the decision makers on what the patient's views would have been had the patient not lacked the requisite mental capacity. The Mental Capacity Act 2005 replaces the common law power to act in the best interests of the patient as set out by the House of Lords in the case of *Re F* [1989].

If David in the above situation was held to be mentally incapacitated then it would be justifiable to tell his wife and daughter of the prognosis. However, temporary incapacity following recovery from an operation would not count as sufficient incapacity to justify the relatives being informed first. If, after a few hours of recovery, it could be anticipated that David would recover his full faculties, then giving information about the diagnosis should be delayed until he could be told and then he could decide how he wished that information to be handled.

Severe harm to the physical or mental health or condition of the patient

The other exception where information may lawfully be withheld is where hearing such news would cause serious harm to the mental or physical health or condition of the patient. The Data Protection Act 1998 (Subject access modification) (Health) Order 2000 SI No 413 (see Appendix 2 to this book) and the Access to Medical Reports Act 1988 (see Chapter 3), which permit access by patients to their health records and (certain) reports, do not permit absolute access. They all recognise that where serious harm would be caused to the applicant then access can be withheld. However, the applicant can challenge such withholding of information and therefore there must be clear reasons based on the particular consequences to that particular patient why access cannot be given.

In other words, the withholding of information cannot be based on a blanket policy, e.g. a policy such as 'in all cases of terminal illness the relatives must be told first'. Each patient must be individually assessed for competence to deal with distressing information. It must not be assumed that simply because information is distressing it automatically would cause serious harm. A similar right of withholding information from patients has been recognised at common law, by the House of Lords, where it was described as the therapeutic privilege of the doctor to withhold information in exceptional situations where consent to treatment was being sought (*Sidaway* v. *Bethlem Royal Hospital Governors*, 1985).

Relatives' annoyance

Many relatives may not know the legal situation and staff are often badgered by relatives for information which is properly the preserve of the patient to be given to them. Relatives do not always wish to protect and promote the autonomy of the patient, and while healthcare professionals are moving away from more paternalistic attitudes in health care, relatives may still be wanting to shield the patient from distressing information and control the communication of such information.

Legal right of relatives to access patient records

In what circumstances, if at all, can relatives ask to see the records of a patient? Under the Data Protection Act 1998 the following persons have rights of access:

- The patient
- A person authorised in writing to make the application on the patient's behalf
- Where the patient is a child (a person under 16 years), a person having parental responsibility for the child (the patient must either consent to the application or the patient must be incapable of understanding and the giving of access would be in his or her best interests)
- Where the patient is incapable of managing his or her own affairs, a person appointed by the court to manage his affairs
- Where the patient has died, the personal representatives of the patient or any person who may have a claim arising out of the patient's death. (Access under this subsection can be prevented if the record includes a note, made at the patient's request, that he or she did not wish access to be given on such an application. Any information need not be disclosed if it is not relevant to any claim which may arise from the patient's death.)

Even when the patient is mentally incapacitated there is no automatic right for a relative to access the records. However, the giving of patient information, as opposed to access to the records, has not in practice kept to such rigid lines and there will be many occasions when information is conveyed by ward staff to relatives on the basis that they are acting in the best interests of that mentally incompetent patient. There are considerable advantages if staff could sensitively learn from patients their views about information being given to relatives if the patient were to become mentally incapable. The patient's wishes could be recorded in the documentation. Information given with the consent of the patient is not a breach of confidentiality.

Conclusion

Staff Nurse Grey could justify her disclosure of information to the relatives if David is mentally incapacitated and the information needs to be given to the relatives in David's best interests, or if the information would be so distressing to David that it would cause serious harm to his physical or mental health. If, on the other hand, David will soon, after recovery from the operation, become mentally competent, and if such information, although distressing, would not in fact cause serious harm, he should be told first. It may of course be David's wish that his wife and daughter are present when he is told, but then such disclosure to them is with his consent.

There should be a regular review of protocols and procedures for those wards and departments which have to communicate such information. Every care should be taken to protect the autonomy of patients so that at this crucial moment of their lives they are not rendered powerless by the withholding from them of possibly the most momentous news they are likely to hear.

References

F v. *West Berkshire Health Authority and another* [1989] 2 All ER 545.
Sidaway v. *Bethlem Royal Hospital Governors* [1985] 1 All ER 643.

CHAPTER 12

The problems posed by suicide and euthanasia

Box 12.1 Case scenario

Jenny White, a hospice nurse, is caring for Peggy who is in the terminal stages of motor neurone disease. Peggy lives at home and is cared for by her husband John with support from the community health team and social services. John confides to Jenny that he has promised his wife that when her suffering becomes unbearable he will help her to end her life. Afterwards, John says he will have no further desire to continue life alone. Should Jenny respect the confidential nature of this information?

Introduction

Nurses who care for patients in distressing situations can become party to many intimate intentions. With those who are terminally ill, the perspectives of both carers and patients can become distorted in the desperate reality of the situation. The difficulty is in empathising with the patient and the relatives while retaining professional detachment in order to provide support and specialist experience. Nurses must understand the legal implications of the situation, so that they are not unwittingly led into criminal activity.

Euthanasia

The UK does not recognise a law permitting euthanasia, whether active or passive, voluntary or involuntary. To deliberately take any action to shorten a patient's life is to commit a crime. Jenny should be aware that John has told her that he intends to commit a crime, i.e. killing his wife. Even though this may be in accordance with Peggy's wishes, to aid and abet the suicide of another is a criminal offence. As a result of the Suicide Act 1961, it is no longer a criminal offence to attempt to commit suicide. However, it remains an offence to assist another person to commit suicide. The changes to the Suicide Act 1961 enacted by the Coroners' and Justice Act 2009 extended the offence of aiding and abetting suicide to encouragement via the internet and did not limit the scope of the offence. If John were to assist his wife to die, he could be prosecuted. If he were to be convicted of murder there would be an automatic sentence of life imprisonment, the mandatory sentence for murder. However, if he were to be convicted of manslaughter the judge has considerable discretion in sentencing. Dr Nigel Cox (*R* v. *Cox* [1992]), who prescribed and administered potassium chloride to a patient who was terminally ill, was given a suspended prison sentence following his conviction for attempted murder. In cases of compassionate killing, relatives in John's situation have been conditionally discharged or given probation. The Coroners and Justice Act 2009 changed the law on defences to a charge of murder by abolishing the common law defence of provocation to a charge of murder. This is replaced by Section 54 which provides a new partial defence of 'loss of control' to a charge of murder. The effect of the defence, if successfully pleaded, is to reduce the charge to one of manslaughter.

In the case of Diane Pretty (*R. (Pretty)* v. *Director of Public Prosecutions* 2001) (see Chapter 2), Mrs Pretty, who was in the terminal stages of motor neurone disease, applied to the High Court for a declaration that, if her husband were to end her life to save her from the suffering and indignity she would otherwise have to endure, he would not be prosecuted under the Suicide Act or other laws. She argued that it was her right under Articles 2, 3, 8, 9 and 14 of the European Convention of Human Rights to die with dignity. The High Court held that the Director of Public Prosecutions did not have the power to give an undertaking not to prosecute a person for the offence of aiding and abetting the suicide of another. The High Court held that the right to life and to dignity did not protect the right to procure one's own death or confer a right to die. Subsequently she took her case to the European Court of Human Rights which stated that there was no incompatibility between the articles of the European Convention on Human Rights and the Suicide Act 1961.

Debbie Purdy, who had multiple sclerosis, challenged the Director of Public Prosecutions (DPP) to reduce the uncertainty as to when there would be a prosecution under the Suicide Act 1961, since she wanted an assurance that, should her husband take her to the Dignitas Clinic in Zurich to end her life, he would not be prosecuted. The House of Lords (*R. (Purdy)* v. *Director of Public Prosecutions* 2009) upheld her application and ordered the DPP to produce guidelines clarifying when there would be a prosecution.

As a consequence, the DPP produced an interim policy on 23 September 2009, which can be seen on the DPP website. The final policy was published in the spring of 2010 following the consultation.

Letting somebody die

The law has been criticised by philosophers on the grounds that it would be more humane to facilitate a speedy death than to let nature take its course. In the Tony Bland case, the House of Lords had to determine whether it was lawful to end artificial feeding for a person in a persistent vegetative state. Tony Bland had not recovered consciousness since his injuries in the Hillsborough football stadium disaster. The dilemma of the situation was recognised by Lord Browne-Wilkinson:

> How can it be lawful to allow a patient to die slowly, though painlessly, over a period of weeks from lack of food but unlawful to produce his immediate death by a lethal injection... it is undoubtedly the law and nothing I have said casts doubt on the proposition that the doing of a positive act with the intention of ending life is and remains murder' (*Airedale NHS Trust* v. *Bland House of Lords* [1993]).

However, in Tony Bland's situation, the House of Lords decided that there was no duty to keep him alive at all costs. Extraordinary treatments could be withheld.

The law distinguishes between a situation where there is no longer a duty in law to keep a person alive at all costs and the patient can be allowed to die, and a situation where action is taken to end the person's life. The former is not criminally wrong; the latter is. Letting Tony Bland die was not a criminal act because ceasing artificial feeding was held to be lawful as there was no duty to keep the patient alive at all costs.

The law also distinguishes between lawful acts such as those designed to reduce pain, which may indirectly reduce the length of life, and unlawful acts such as deliberately giving a patient a drug to speed death. Dr Bodkin Adams was found not guilty of causing the death of a resident in an Eastbourne nursing home when he prescribed morphine for her care. The judge, Mr Justice Patrick Devlin, directed the jury that although a doctor cannot deliberately end a life, the treatment given in this case was designed to promote comfort. Therefore, life was incidentally shortened and there were no grounds for a murder conviction (*R* v. *Bodkin Adams* 1957). This ruling still applies today.

Summary of the legal principles

If John were to bring Peggy's life to an end, even though Peggy gave her consent, John would be guilty of an offence. If he were then to attempt suicide, and failed, he could not be prosecuted for the attempt on his life.

Confidentiality

Jenny has a duty of confidentiality to Peggy and John and it is only if one of the recognised exceptions to this duty arises that Jenny would be justified in passing on the information.

John's intention to end Peggy's life

Despite the circumstances this is a criminal act. However, the law does not require a practitioner to inform the police of every crime they come across. There are statutes requiring disclosure of information, but they are unusual. For example, the Road Traffic Act requires notification if there is a road accident leading to personal injury and the Prevention of Terrorism Acts require notification of any terrorist activities. The NMC recognises that there may be an exception to the duty of confidentiality where it is in the public interest for confidential information to be disclosed. This was considered in Chapter 2.

It could be argued that what happens between John and Peggy is a private matter; if they decide upon a suicide pact, that is their concern. However, the problems which John and Peggy are confronting are of considerable public significance. Society has a role to support those who find themselves in this situation. Could more be done to support Peggy in order that John does not feel that he has to end her life? Should Jenny be assisting the couple by bringing in expert counselling, improved pain relief, speech therapy (to assist in any dysphagia problems) and other specialist help? What would be seen as the reasonable standard of practice for a nurse in Jenny's situation?

John's intention to end his life

While suicide is not a crime, similar issues are raised in relation to John's feeling that he does not want to survive Peggy's death as are raised by her terminal condition. Support should be available to John to show him that there could be a future for him after Peggy's death, e.g. counselling and assistance from those who have suffered in similar circumstances.

Conclusion

This is a difficult area of law since there is no clear statute or case law covering the duty of confidentiality, and the exceptions to it, in circumstances such as these. The basic principles have to be identified and then applied to the particular facts.

One way of arriving at an answer to Jenny's legal situation is to imagine that she respected the confidentiality of John's intention, and that John ended Peggy's life but failed in an attempt to end his own. John could then be prosecuted for causing Peggy's death. If it were proved that Jenny had been aware of the situation and failed to take action, she would put herself at risk of being found guilty of professional misconduct in failing to notify the appropriate persons and in failing to secure more help and support for Peggy and John. The NMC (2008) requires every practitioner to make the care of people your first concern, treating them as individuals and respecting their dignity. Jenny could even risk being accused of involvement in the actual killing if she were aware of John's plan and failed to take action, since her actions may be construed as amounting to aiding and abetting the suicide.

The solution must favour Jenny passing information on to the appropriate colleagues in order to secure support for the couple. Ideally, she should discuss her concerns with John and Peggy, if Peggy is mentally capable of being involved, and also obtain John's consent to the confidential information being made known. In this way there would be no breach of confidentiality since the person's consent to the disclosure would be a complete defence to any action relating to the disclosure. The importance of Jenny's record keeping in this dilemma cannot be emphasised enough. A similar situation is considered in George and Dimond (2009).

References

Airedale NHS Trust v. *Bland H.L.* [1993] 1 All ER 821.

George, R. and Dimond, B. (2009) Suicide: the legal and ethical aspects. *End of Life Journal*, **3**(4), 26–30.

Nursing and Midwifery Council (2008) *The Code: Standards of Conduct, Performance and Ethics for Nurses and Midwives*. NMC, London.

R v. *Bodkin Adams* [1957] Crim LR 365.

R v. *Cox* [1992] The Times 22 September.

R. (Pretty) v. *Director of Public Prosecutions and Another*, Medical Ethics Alliance and Others, interveners Times Law Report 23 October, 2001; [2001] UKHL 61; [2001] 3 WLR 1598; [2002] 1 All ER 1; *Pretty* v. *UK* [2002] ECHR 427.

R. (Purdy) v. *Director of Public Prosecutions* The Times Law Report 31 July 2009 HL.

CHAPTER 13

The rights of transplant recipients and donors

Box 13.1 Case scenario

Staff Nurse Fawn works on a transplant unit and is approached by a journalist who is seeking to write a report on a recent transplant success. Nurse Fawn knows that the recipient patient is happy to be interviewed, but the journalist wants her to find out the name and address of the donor family, so that the public can have both sides of the story.

Introduction

Transplant surgery is one of the medical miracles of the last decade and is clearly highly newsworthy. Almost every day there are news items about amazing transplant successes: sometimes generous relatives are reported as donating a kidney or part of a liver or even part of a lung; sometimes strangers have benefited from the final act of a dying person who was carrying a donor card; and sometimes relatives struggling to come to terms with bereavement have still been prepared to agree to organ donation. Such situations give rise to very special issues relating to confidentiality. This chapter explores the legal situation.

The transplant situation: two different perspectives

Where organs are donated after death to unrelated persons, two different families are linked in very different circumstances. The donor family is grieving, often after a very sudden death, frequently of a young person. The shock, the sadness, and the feelings of waste and futility dominate their thoughts. The possibility of ever adjusting to that loss and carrying on with ordinary life must seem inconceivable. Into this context comes the request for organs to be donated.

If organ donation takes place, the family and their friends still have to cope with the bereavement and the added worry that the transplant may fail, and thus they could face a sense of a second loss and bereavement.

On the other hand, the recipient patient and his or her family have, for a considerable length of time, had to face the imminent possibility of death. They have been told that only a transplant can save the patient's life. The patient may have been placed on a waiting list for many months or even years. Then suddenly the call comes: organs are available and the patient is rushed to the hospital for preoperative checks and in for the transplant to take place. Patient and relatives are, of course, nervous, but there is an anticipation that at last there is a chance of life; they are looking to the future with hope, joy and happiness. Therefore one family is looking at the past and the other at the future.

The law on consent and transplants from a deceased person

The Human Tissue Act 2004 distinguishes between two situations: one where the deceased has made clear his or her wishes to be a donor and possibly carried a card; the second where the deceased has not expressed any wishes and consent to the donation must be obtained in other ways.

In the first situation, the relatives have no legal right to prevent the donation of organs. The Code of Practice issued by the Human Tissue Authority (2006) should be followed. The Code suggests that:

They (relatives) should be encouraged to accept the deceased person's wishes and it should be made clear that they do not have the legal right to veto or overrule those wishes. There may nevertheless be cases in which donation is inappropriate and each case should be considered individually.

In the second situation, the Human Tissue Act 2004 sets out a hierarchy for consent to be obtained. At the top of this hierarchy is any person nominated as a personal representative by the deceased; in the absence of such a nomination, consent can be given by a person who is in a qualifying relationship with the deceased immediately before the death. Section 27(4) of the Human Tissue

Act 2004 sets out the order of priority of such persons, with a spouse or partner (including civil or same sex partner) as the top priority.

The general principles

The basic principles of confidentiality apply to the two situations. Both families are entitled to have the donation and the transplant kept confidential. If the recipient patient consents to information being given to the press, then this is without prejudice to the right of the donor family to remain completely anonymous and their address and details kept secret and vice versa.

It would be rare for any of the exceptions to the duty of confidentiality discussed in this book to apply in this situation. However, disclosure as a result of the order of the court (see Chapter 4) (e.g. if litigation was brought by the recipient or his or her family alleging breach of the duty of care by the surgeon or even the donor's family) or in the public interest (see Chapter 2) (e.g. if an infectious disease had been passed on (see Chapter 5)) may in exceptional circumstances be justified.

The official policy

Transplant coordinators, who link professionals in the hospital at which the donor is being cared for with the professionals at the hospital at which the transplant will take place, work under very clear guidance. It is the official policy that the instructions of the donor family should be taken in relation to subsequent communication. If the family has requested anonymity and has also stated that they do not wish to receive any contact or communication from the recipient, then those wishes must be respected. Even if the recipient wishes a letter of thanks to be conveyed to the donor family, it will not be delivered if the donor family has expressed a wish for no contact.

All communications should be made via the transplant coordinator. Neither family should put their own name and address on communications. In this way, contact, where not prohibited, can be made through the coordinator, and the donor family can have information about the progress of the recipients. If either party subsequently want to make themselves known to the other, then this can be negotiated through the transplant coordinator. Therefore, transplant coordinators have a key role to play in sensitively passing on messages and facilitating the limited communication which is required.

What if the recipient fails to follow the rules?

Box 13.2 Case scenario 2

Polly, a sufferer from cystic fibrosis, had a heart–lung transplant and was told nothing about the donor and had no idea who he or she was, or where in the country the donor came from. However, on returning home from hospital, Polly wrote a letter of thanks to the donor family, sending it to the transplant coordinator at the hospital. Polly put her name and address on the letter. Although she had been told that this should not be done, she felt that it would be a poor letter of thanks if she was not prepared to put her name and address on the letter. Polly did not expect a reply because she knew it was the right of the family to request no contact. However, about a month later, she had a reply from the mother of the 16-year-old boy who had died in a road accident. As a consequence, correspondence between Polly and donor family started and led to their meeting up. Fortunately, the donor family said that they benefited from the contact with Polly and the knowledge that their son's death was not in vain.

In the case scenario of Box 13.2 clearly the donor family were able to handle the different situations of their family compared with Polly's family, but things might have turned out differently, with considerable stress for both families resulting from the contact. For this reason the official policy is in favour of anonymity of both parties.

Answering the question posed

In the case scenario Staff Nurse Fawn should refer the journalist to the transplant coordinator. She should give no information out about the recipient patient, even though the patient is consenting to the disclosure of the information. It is preferable for the transplant coordinator to have the responsibility for any communication with the press and, where the families are willing to be made known, for the transplant coordinator to work with the press office of the trust to channel such information and protect the families from harassment.

Conclusion

The usual rules of confidentiality apply to a transplant situation, and because of media interest, every effort must be made to protect both families from pressure to disclose information. Only if one of the recognised grounds for breaching confidentiality were to apply, such as the consent of those concerned or an order from the court, could information about the transplant be disclosed.

References

Human Tissue Authority (2006) *Code of Practice: Donation of Organs, Tissue and Cells for Transplantation Code 2*. The Stationery Office, London.

Powers of the police and access to information

Introduction

A powerful reciprocal relationship often develops between A&E staff and the local police. The latter are at hand to arrest and tackle those who are violent towards A&E staff, especially at the weekends when alcohol is a factor. In turn, the nursing staff may feel under pressure to provide confidential information to police to assist them in making arrests and bringing charges against those who are guilty of violence.

Before the attempt to commit suicide was decriminalised under the Suicide Act 1961, police would attempt to obtain details of those who had failed to kill themselves in order that a prosecution could be brought. There are, however, dangers in this reciprocal relationship between A&E staff and the police, since the duty of confidentiality owed by nurses to their patients may be broken without justification.

This chapter deals with what healthcare professionals are legally obliged to tell the police and when the police can request sight of medical records and obtain blood or urine samples.

Police and Criminal Evidence Act 1984

The police have no general powers to compel hospital staff to produce any information which they consider is relevant to their purpose. The healthcare professional's duty of confidentiality is respected, but the Police and Criminal Evidence Act 1984 (PACE 1984) (Kennedy and Grubb, 2000) sets out a procedure for personal health information that can be accessed by the police. Police do not have a right to search and access personal records unless special provisions are complied with. Personal records include records relating to an individual (whether living or dead) which could identify that individual and/or relate to his or her physical or mental health or to his or her (spiritual) counselling or assistance. Access to personal records can be obtained if the special procedure set out in schedule 1 to PACE 1984 is followed. It covers information which is acquired in the course of a trade, business or profession and which is held subject to an express or implied term that it should be held in confidence.

Human tissue or tissue fluid which has been taken for the purposes of diagnosis or medical treatment is excluded material and must be held in confidence by all staff. Police have to have specific powers and follow the special procedure if they want access to excluded material.

Special procedure for access

A constable can apply to a circuit judge and if the latter is satisfied that one or other of two sets of access conditions is fulfilled (Tables 14.1 and 14.2),

Table 14.1 First set of access conditions.

The first set of access conditions apply if there are reasonable grounds for believing that:

- A serious arrestable offence has been committed
- There is special procedure material, but not excluded material
- The material is likely to be of substantial value in the investigation
- The material is likely to be relevant evidence
- Other methods of obtaining the material have been tried without success
- It is in the public interest that the material should be produced or that access should be given

Table 14.2 Second set of access conditions.

An intimate sample can be taken if there are reasonable grounds:

- For suspecting the involvement of the person from whom the sample is to be taken in a serious arrestable offence

- For believing the sample will tend to confirm or disprove his/her involvement

then the judge can make an order requiring a person who appears to be in possession of the material to produce it. The constable must then have access to the material not later than seven days from the date of the order or any other specified period.

If the possessor of the material fails to comply with the order and produce the information or permit access to it, then the judge, if he or she is satisfied that the access conditions exist and the order has not been complied with, can issue a warrant authorising the constable to enter and search the premises. The judge can also deal with the offender as if he or she were in contempt of court.

Guidance from the Nursing and Midwifery Council

In answering the question 'What information must be disclosed to the police?' the NMC (2009) in its guidance states that:

In English law there is no obligation placed upon any citizen to answer questions put to them by the police. However, there are some exceptional situations in which disclosure is required by statute. These include:

- the duty to report notifiable diseases in accordance with the Public Health Act 1984
- the duty to inform the Police, when asked, of the name and address of drivers who are allegedly guilty of an offence contrary to the Road Traffic Act 1998
- the duty not to withhold information relating to the commission of acts of terrorism contrary to the Terrorism Act 2000
- the duty to report relevant infectious diseases in accordance with the Public Health (Infectious Diseases) Regulations 1988

The NMC points out that the police have no automatic right to demand access to a person's medical records. Usually, before the police may examine a person's records they must obtain a warrant under the Police and Criminal

Evidence Act 1984. Before a police constable can gain access to a hospital, for example, in order to search for information such as medical records or samples of human tissue, he or she must apply to a circuit judge for a warrant. The police have no duty to inform the person whose confidential information is sought, but must inform the person holding that information.

Guidance from the Department of Health

In Annex C of the Code of Practice on Confidentiality published by the Department of Health (2003), guidance is provided on the disclosure of information to the police:

> Whilst the police have no general right of access to health records there are a number of statutes which require disclosure to them and some that permit disclosure. These have the effect of making disclosure a legitimate function in the circumstances they cover.
>
> In the absence of a requirement to disclose there must be either explicit patient consent or a robust public interest justification. What is or isn't in the public interest is ultimately decided by the Courts.

Where disclosure is justified it should be limited to the minimum necessary to meet the need and patients should be informed of the disclosure unless it would defeat the purpose of the investigation, allow a potential criminal to escape or put staff or others at risk.

The definition of 'serious crime' used by the DH is discussed in Chapter 2 on public interest.

Voluntary disclosure of confidential information

Many health organisations would not wait for an order from a circuit judge before making information available to the police. Where it is clear that a health organisation has information that is relevant to a police investigation and for which disclosure is justified in the public interest (on the grounds that it involves a serious threat to the health and safety of an individual) then this limited information can be made available voluntarily (*R* v. *Singleton* [1994]). For example, if the police are able to give a detailed description of the person wanted in connection with a serious arrestable offence and that person has received treatment in the A&E department, then that information could be given to the police.

However, the police would not be permitted to look through the records of all persons treated that day in the hope that they might identify a possible suspect. If there is doubt over the category that any particular set of records comes into, then it would probably be wiser to refuse disclosure. The DH has advised that disclosure of confidential information to the police in serious criminal cases such as murder, manslaughter and rape would be justified (DH, 2003). The British Medical Association (BMA) has prepared a toolkit of guidance on disclosing confidential information which includes disclosure to the police (BMA, 2008). The toolkit aims to identify the key factors which have to be taken into account when making decisions about disclosure.

Many A&E departments have arrangements which circumvent the necessity of the police obtaining an order from a circuit judge. These arrangements recognise the duty of confidentiality of the staff and the narrow exception of disclosure in the public interest. These local arrangements should be recorded in a procedure which guides both police and A&E staff. The procedure should contain details of the resolution of any disputes between A&E departments and the police.

Health care professionals as witnesses

If the police are investigating a crime and ask questions of a healthcare professional as part of that investigation, then the practitioner would be obliged to answer honestly and fully any questions put to him or her. The fact that some of the information relates to confidential patient material may provide a lawful excuse, and therefore defence, for not answering those questions (*Rice* v. *Connolly* [1966]). As a potential witness he or she would be expected to provide a statement to the police. In such circumstances, it would be advisable for the practitioner to obtain the assistance of a senior manager or lawyer to the health organisation before making the statement, especially if confidential information were required.

Where questions are asked in court, the practitioner is unable to rely upon any justification for not disclosing information on the grounds that it was confidential (see Chapter 4).

Road traffic offences and the Prevention of Terrorism Act

These statutes involve a duty to provide information to the police. Thus, following a road accident which has led to personal injuries it would be a criminal offence for a health professional to refuse to notify the police of the name and address of those involved in the accident (*Hunter* v. *Mann* [1974]).

Similarly, any person finding evidence of terrorist activity (e.g. the location of weapons) has a clear duty to report this to the police. Failure to do so is a criminal offence.

Intimate samples

Section 65 of PACE 1984 defines an intimate sample as: 'A sample of blood, semen, or any other tissue fluid, urine, saliva or pubic hair, or a swab taken from a person's body orifice'. The taking of intimate samples by the police is covered under section 62 of PACE 1984. This enables an intimate sample to be taken from a person in police detention if the police officer of at least superintendent rank authorises it to be taken and the appropriate consent has been given. It can only be authorised if the conditions set out in Table 14.3 are satisfied.

The authorisation can be given orally, but must be confirmed in writing. The consent of the person in detention must be given in writing and he or she must be told of the authorisation and the grounds for giving it, including the nature of the offence of which he or she is suspected. All this information must be recorded by the police. Apart from urine and saliva, an intimate sample can only be taken by a registered medical practitioner.

It should be noted that consent in writing is an express requirement of the legality of taking any intimate samples. In some circumstances it can be an offence not to provide a sample, thus under road traffic legislation it is an offence to refuse to supply a sample of breath, blood or urine in drink-driving cases. In other cases, refusal to provide a sample can lead to an inference of guilt.

Non-intimate samples

Non-intimate samples (Table 14.4) can be taken without consent under section 63(3) of PACE 1984 if the person is in police detention or held in police

Table 14.3 Conditions for authorising the taking intimate samples.

If there are reasonable grounds:

- for suspecting the involvement of the person from whom the sample is to be taken in a serious arrestable offence; and
- for believing the sample will tend to confirm or disprove his involvement

Table 14.4 Definition of a non-intimate sample.

- Sample of hair other than pubic hair
- Sample taken from a nail or from under a nail
- Swab taken from any part of a person's body other than a body orifice
- A footprint or a similar impression of any part of a person's body other than part of his or her hand

custody and an officer of at least the rank of superintendent authorises it to be taken.

Involvement of health professionals in taking samples

If the patient refused to provide an intimate sample, it would be unlawful for a health professional to give to the police a sample which had been taken for other purposes, e.g. diagnosis.

Reporting gunshot and knife wounds

The GMC (2009) has supplemented its guidance on confidentiality with guidance on reporting gunshot and knife wounds. The guidance describes a two-stage process:

(a) You should inform the police quickly whenever a person arrives with a gunshot wound or an injury from an attack with a knife, blade or other sharp instrument. This will enable the police to make an assessment of risk to the patient and others, and to gather statistical information about gun and knife crime in the area

(b) You should make a professional judgment about whether disclosure of personal information about a patient, including their identity, is justified in the public interest.

The police are responsible for assessing the risk posed by a member of the public who is armed with, and has used, a gun or knife in a violent attack. They need to consider:

   (a) the risk of a further attack on the patient

   (b) the risk to staff, patients and visitors in the A&E department or hospital, and

   (c) the risk of another attack near to, or at, the site of the original incident.

The guidance emphasises the importance of obtaining the patient's consent to the disclosure where this is practicable and also the importance of documenting the reasons for any disclosure and the action taken.

The GMC guidance also covers the situation relating to any young person under 18 arriving with a gunshot wound or a wound from an attack with a knife, blade or other sharp instrument. The child protection concerns which arise should lead to the doctor informing an appropriate person or authority promptly of any such incident. If the injury from a knife or blade is accidental or the result of self-harm, there would usually be no duty to inform the police.

Case scenario

Paula should be able to refer to a local procedure regarding her duty to supply information to the police. It is likely that this procedure would state that the prior approval of the consultant in charge of the A&E department should be obtained before the disclosure of confidential information to the police.

In these specific circumstances, if the police had a fairly full description of the assailant, then the consultant might be justified in disclosing to the police the fact that a man meeting that description has been treated in the A&E department and pass on to the police details of that person's name and address. Handing the police the records of all people treated in the A&E department that day or the previous night would not be justified.

Conclusion

Health professionals have to walk a tightrope between the public interest in securing health and safety and the rights of the patient to have information kept confidential. The advice given by the NMC, HPC and GMC, and the Codes of Practice of other health professionals as appropriate, should be followed and comprehensive records kept of the police visit and the action taken.

References

British Medical Association (2008) *Confidentiality and Disclosure of Information Toolkit*. BMA, London.

Department of Health (2003) *Confidentiality: NHS Code of Practice*. DH, London.

General Medical Council (2009) *Confidentiality: Reporting Gun Shots and Knife Wounds*. GMC, London.

Hunter v. *Mann* [1974] QB 767.

Kennedy, I. and Grubb, A. (2000) *Medical Law Text with Materials*. Butterworth, London.

Nursing and Midwifery Council (2009) *Advice Sheet: Confidentiality (A to Z Guidance)*. NMC, London.

R v. *Singleton* [1994] The Times Law Report 22 June.

Rice v. *Connolly* [1966] 2 All ER 649.

CHAPTER 15

Child protection and unsuitable employees

Box 15.1 Case scenario

Mavis Brown learned that Bob Downs was applying for the post of care assistant to work in the paediatric ward. She knew him from her home town where he had a reputation as a child abuser. What action should she take?

Introduction

In Chapter 10 of this book it was established that the protection of a child is a significant exception to the duty of confidentiality. If the safety or health or welfare of the child is endangered then any person would be justified in the public interest in ensuring that appropriate action was taken to safeguard the interests of that child, even though this entailed a breach of the duty of confidentiality.

This chapter looks at the statutory provisions for checking on the suitability for people to work with children. The Department of Health (DH) and other organisations have issued guidance on interagency cooperation (DH *et al.*, 1999). The chapter also discusses The Sexual Offenders Act 1997, its provisions and the extent to which people can access information contained on the Register. The Rehabilitation of Offenders Act 1974 does not apply to those who work in health services, so previous offences would have to be disclosed when seeking employment as a care assistant.

The Protection of Children Act 1999

This Act had four purposes (Table 15.1).

Table 15.1 Purposes of the Protection of Children Act 1999.

- It makes statutory the Department of Health's consultancy service index list and it requires child care organisations to refer the names of individuals considered unsuitable to work with children for inclusion on the list.

- It provides rights of appeal against inclusion.

- It requires regulated childcare organisations to check the names of anyone they propose to employ in posts involving regular contact with children with the list and not to employ them if listed.

- It amends part V of the Police Act 1997 to allow the Criminal Records Bureau to act as a central access point for criminal records information, List 99[1] and the new Department of Health list. In other words, the Criminal Records Bureau was to act as a one-stop shop in the carrying out of checks.

[1]List 99 is a list held by the Department for Education and Employment of those considered unsuitable to work with children. It has always been a statutory list.

The Act also provides for an independent appeal system. The Act defines a 'childcare organisation' as being concerned with the provision of accommodation, social services, or health services to children, where the activities are regulated by legislation. The definition includes all local authority social services functions relating to children, all children's homes – whether local authority, private or independent – nursing homes accommodating children, registered child minders and some NHS trust services for children. Clearly, a NHS trust with paediatric services comes under the provisions of this legislation. The effect of the legislation is that such organisations have a statutory duty to vet prospective employees, paid or unpaid, for work involving contact with children.

Care Standards Act 2000

Under Part VII of the Care Standards Act statutory provisions was made for setting up a list of individuals who are considered unsuitable to work with vulnerable adults. A single list was established for both England and Wales and it operated in a similar way to the list established under the Protection of Children Act 1999. It now comes under the Independent Safeguarding Authority, which is discussed below.

The Safeguarding Vulnerable Groups Act 2006

This Act aimed at strengthening current safeguarding arrangements for individuals in the workplace and reducing the risk of individuals suffering harm at the hands of those employed in either paid or voluntary capacity to work with them. The Independent Barring Board (IBB) was set up on 2 January 2008 and people included in lists maintained under the Protection of Children Act 1999 or the Care Standards Act 2000 or who are subject to a direction under the Education Act 2002 Section 142 were included or considered for inclusion by the IBB in the children's barred list of the adults' barred lists.

The IBB was renamed the Independent Safeguarding Authority (ISA; http:// www.isa-gov.org.uk/) which was established to support the implementation of the Safeguarding Vulnerable Groups Act and bring together the existing barring schemes, Protection of Vulnerable Adults (POVA), Protection of Children Act and List 99. From the autumn of 2008 ISA covered the following areas:

- Coverage of all workforce areas where children or vulnerable adults may be exposed to abuse or exploited instead of just regulated social care settings
- Pre-employment vetting
- Independent and consistent decision-making by employers
- Continuous monitoring: ISA can review decision not to bar on receipt of new information
- Reduction in bureaucracy: on line and free of charge checking system, once people have joined the scheme
- Wide range of sources of information: duty of employers and service providers to give information to the scheme
- Coverage across the UK

ISA issued a consultation paper on the barring process in June 2007 covering the time period for making representations; the minimum no-review period; the age boundary in relation to the minimum barred period and automatic barring offences. It was estimated that 11 million individuals would have to be passed through the ISA's checking process in the first five years of its operations.

Vetting and Barring Scheme

From 12 October 2009 the ISA responsibilities for barring individuals who pose a known risk from working or volunteering with children and vulnerable adults were further strengthened as more sectors such as the NHS and the Prison Service came under the Scheme and new criminal offences came into force. The Home Office introduced increased safeguards under the new Vetting and Barring Scheme (VBS) delivered by the Independent Safeguarding Authority (ISA) and the CRB. The new scheme was created following the Bichard Inquiry into the Soham murders. Tighter regulations were at the heart of the Government's strategy for increasing protection of vulnerable members of our society. The following increased safeguards were introduced:

- It is a criminal offence for barred individuals to apply to work with children or vulnerable adults in a wide range of posts.
- Employers face criminal penalties if they knowingly permit barred individuals to engage in Regulated Activity.
- The three current barring lists (POVA, POCA and List 99) were replaced by the creation of two new barred lists administered by the ISA. Checks of these two lists can be made as part of an Enhanced CRB check.
- Additional jobs and voluntary positions are covered by the barring arrangements, including moderators of children's internet chat rooms and a large number of NHS and prison service staff.
- Employers, social services and professional regulators have a duty to refer to the ISA any information about individuals who may pose a risk to children and vulnerable adults.

In addition there were also a number of changes to the way that applications for CRB checks were to be made. A check of the new ISA barred lists is only available as part of an Enhanced CRB check:

- An Enhanced CRB check is required for positions involving work with children and vulnerable adults.
- Eligibility for Enhanced CRB checks extends to include anyone working in Regulated Activity with a Regulated Activity provider.
- The POVA First service is renamed ISA Adult First (https://www.isaadult-first.co.uk/guidance.aspx).

A phasing strategy will eventual cover all existing staff who require an Enhanced CRB check.

Further details on the Vetting and Barring Scheme can be found on the Home Office website (http://www.crb.homeoffice.gov.uk/faqs/vetting_and_barring_scheme.aspx).

Changes were made to these tougher measures introduced in October 2009 following protests from such well known authors as Philip Pullman, who under the new regime would be required to undergo a check before speaking in a school.

The Department for Children, Schools and Families (DCSF) has also developed a cross-government strategy for children and young people called 'Staying Safe' which can be accessed on the DCSF website and the police website (http://police.homeoffice.gov.uk/operational-policing/safeguarding-vulnerable-persons/safeguarding/).

What should Mavis do?

Mavis has a duty to her employers to ensure that the appropriate checks are made about Bob as a prospective employee. (They should have checked even without Mavis' prompting.) They would apply to the Independent Safeguarding Authority to find out if Bob is listed. If he is listed, then he cannot be employed by the organisation to work with children. However, it may well be that when investigations are made Bob Downs is not on any list of sexual offenders and there are no clear facts, just rumours, about his child abuse activities. What action should Mavis take? In the absence of any clear information about Bob's potential danger to children, Mavis would have little justification in reporting him to senior management. However she may be able to check that the procedures recommended by the Clothier Report following the crimes of Beverly Allitt are in place, so that precautions are taken to prevent harm to patients from employees (Allitt Enquiry, 1994).

What are Bob's rights?

Bob has the right of appeal. An independent review tribunal will review the way in which the decisions by the DH to place the individual on the list have been reached (i.e. a review confined solely to procedure). It will also examine the evidence afresh and make its own decision on the merits of the particular case.

Information Commissioner's checklist

The setting up of a Register which contains personal information about child protection could be a breach of data protection legislation unless specific principles are followed (DH *et al.*, 1999, appendix 4). These include the requirements that:

- There must be a legitimate purpose to hold the data, with a restriction on secondary use of the material
- The information must be shared in order for that purpose to be fulfilled
- The parties concerned have the legal power to disclose the personal information for that purpose
- The extent of the information held is necessary for the purpose
- Either the consent of the individual has been obtained or there is an overriding public interest or justification for disclosing the information
- The disclosure comes under the exemptions recognised by the Data Protection Acts 1984 and 1998 (e.g. prevention or detection of a crime)
- Compliance with other data protection principles is secured (see Chapter 3) covering the minimum amount of data necessary, the accuracy, the length of time it is retained, access by individuals, and its storage

The Court of Appeal ruled that the list maintained by the DH of people who were thought unsuitable to work with children was neither unlawful nor was it operated unreasonably (*R* v. *Secretary of State for Health ex parte C* [2000]).

The Sexual Offenders Act 1997

The Sexual Offenders Act 1997 was passed in order to ensure that once a sex offender had served his sentence and was about to be released, he would still be subject to some form of supervision to protect persons against the risk of his reoffending. Part 1 of the Act requires the notification of information to the police by persons who have committed certain sexual offences.

How long do the provisions of notification apply?

Section 1(4) sets out a table giving the time limits for the application of the notification provisions. These vary from an indefinite period for persons who have been sentenced to life imprisonment or for a term of 30 months or more in respect of one of the specified offences to a minimum of a period of 5 years following the conviction or the finding. Thus, those guilty of the most serious crimes will remain on the register till death. Those sent to prison for between 6 and 30 months will remain on the register for 10 years. Sections 1(5) and (6) cover the situation where a person is convicted of several offences to which the part 1 provisions apply.

What is required by the notification provisions?

A person who comes under the offence provisions set out in section 1 and schedule 1 is required, before the end of the period of 14 days beginning with the relevant date or, if later, the commencement of this part, to notify the police of the following information: his name, and, where he also uses one or more other names, each of those names; and his home address (S2(1)). In addition, under section 2(2) the person must notify the police of any change of his name or change of his home address, or any premises where he has resided for a qualifying period. The notification to the police must also include his date of birth, his name on the relevant date, and his home address on that date. Any time when the person is remanded or committed to custody by order of court, is serving a sentence of imprisonment, is detained in hospital, or is outside the UK, is disregarded in determining any relevant period of time.

How is notification made?

The individual can give notification by attending at a police station in his local police area and giving an oral notification to any police officer, or to any person authorised for the purpose by the officer in charge of the station. Alternatively, the individual can send a written notification to any such police station (S2(5)). The notification must be acknowledged in writing and the Secretary of State can direct the form of the acknowledgement.

Consequences of failing to comply with notification provisions

Any person under a duty to make a notification who fails, without reasonable cause, to comply is guilty of an offence. So also is a person who provides any information which he knows to be false (S3(1)).

Young offenders

Section 4 applies the provisions of part 1 to those sentences being served by young offenders. The period during which notification is required is halved for those under 18 years (S4(2)). Parents can be directed by the court to fulfil the notification provisions for certain offenders who are under 18 years, until they become 18.

Home Office guidance

The Home Office issued guidance in 1997. It provides a summary of the Act, sources for additional information, format of the official acknowledgement form, notice of requirement to register, and certification of conviction or finding. Appendix A sets out interim guidance on the way in which police forces should manage the information they receive about sex offenders subject to the Act and the criteria which should govern those decisions. An annex to Appendix A summarises some of the cases relevant to police disclosure. Appendix B provides supplementary guidance on the new requirements, the cautioning of a sex offender, the statutory forms, and the treatment of mentally disordered offenders under the Act.

Implementation of the Act and confidentiality

The Sex Offenders Act 1997 came into force on 1 September 1997 (The Sex Offenders Act 1997 (Commencement Order) 1997 Statutory Instrument 1997, No 1920). There have been concerns over who had access to the Register kept by the police, e.g. could neighbours be told when a sex offender moves into the area? The guidance issued by the Home Office (1997) cites a case (*R* v. *Chief Constable of North Wales Police ex parte AB* [1997]) (Box 15.2) where it was held that in certain circumstances disclosure about offenders by the police to third parties was justifiable, but blanket disclosure policies were objectionable and any decision to disclose must depend upon a careful consideration of the facts of the case.

Box 15.2 *R* v. *Chief Constable of North Wales Police ex parte AB* [1997]

Following their release from prison after serving long sentences for sexual offences against children, AB and CD, a married couple, moved to the North of England and later to a caravan site in North Wales. After receiving a report from Northumbrian police, the North Wales police asked them to move on before Easter, when a large number of children

---

were expected to visit the caravan site. They refused and the police then showed the caravan site owner material about the couple which had appeared in the local press. The owner then asked the couple to leave which they did. The couple applied for judicial review of the action of the police.

It was held that where the police obtain information about a member of the public it should not be disclosed except for the purpose and to the degree necessary to fulfil their public duties. This principle did not arise from a duty of confidence owed to the police to a member of the public, but from a fundamental rule of good public administration. However, if the police, after careful consideration, determined that it was desirable or necessary in the public interest to disclose information to prevent crime or alert the public to a particular danger, it would be proper to make such limited disclosure as was necessary to achieve that purpose.

However, any NHS trust officer who enquired of the Register about persons moving to the locality of a children's ward would probably come within the range of justifiable disclosure. The contents of the Register cannot, therefore, be automatically made available to any interested persons: the police, who are its custodians, have to exercise discrimination about to whom specific entries are notified.

DNA databases

A recent case came before the European Court of Human Rights concerning the National DNA database. Two men from Sheffield, Michael Marper and S., brought the case because they were arrested in 2001 and had their fingerprints and DNA samples taken. They were not convicted of any crime and argued that the samples should have been destroyed. Their case was rejected by the British courts and in February 2008 the ECHR gave permission for the case to proceed (*Marper* v. *UK* [2007]). The ECHR subsequently held that storage of DNA profiles of suspects who were not convicted was a breach of Article 8 and constituted a disproportionate interference with the applicants' right to privacy (*S. and Marper* v. *UK* [2008]). The ECHR considered that the blanket and indiscriminate nature of the powers given to the police could not be regarded as necessary in a democratic society. As a consequence of this judgment more than 1.6 million DNA and fingerprint samples had to be destroyed from police databases.

Conclusions

This whole area is fraught with legal problems. On the one hand there is a duty to ensure that the welfare of the child is the paramount consideration. On the other hand, individuals should not unjustly be prevented from working with children if the evidence does not support a prohibition. Their rights to freedom to work would be protected by the Human Rights Act 1998. The Independent Safeguarding Authority (ISA) has a major task to carry out in undertaking the necessary checks to protect children and vulnerable adults and it would be unfortunate if its work failed to be supported by the general public because the checks were seen as unnecessarily onerous and of little value.

References

Allitt Inquiry (1994) Chaired by Sir Cecil Clothier. HMSO, London.

Home Office (1997) HOC 39/1997. *Sex Offenders Act 1997*. For copies and further information apply to Sentencing and Offences Unit, Home Office, London.

Home Office, Department for Education and Employment, National Assembly for Wales (1999) *Working Together to Safeguard Children*. DH, London.

Marper v. *UK* [2007] EHCR 110; application nos 30562/04 and 30566/04.

R v. *Chief Constable of North Wales Police ex parte AB* [1997] The Times 14 July 1997, Current Law 460 August 1997.

R v. *Secretary of State for Health ex parte C* [2000]. TLR, 1 March 2000.

S. and Marper v. *UK* (Application Nos 30562/04 and 30566/04 ECHR [2008] The Times 8 December 2008 [2008] ECHR 1581

CHAPTER 16

Conclusions

The second edition of this book has covered a wide range of situations and laws relating to confidentiality but it cannot claim to have covered every conceivable situation which is likely to arise. It is hoped that sufficient information has been given about the basic principles and legislation so that the health professional can apply these to any specific situation which arises. Individual practitioners should be aware of the professional advice contained in their code of professional conduct and ensure that they keep up to date with any changes in the law or professional guidance. Inevitably there are many situations which are not black and white, where the practitioner has to use professional discretion to determine whether the duty of confidentiality should prevail over any demands for disclosure or whether the situation comes within a legally recognised justification of an exception to the duty of confidentiality. As in so many areas of professional practice, it is vital that the situation, the decision made and the justifications for that decision are carefully documented. The report of the Bristol Inquiry (Bristol Royal Infirmary, 2001) has urged that there should be respect and honesty at the heart of healthcare and that there should be a partnership between patient and health professional. There are now in place statutory measures to ensure that staff are supported. If there are concerns, staff have the protection of the Public Interest Disclosure Act (see Chapter 9) in making a justified disclosure. In every NHS organisation there should be a person at senior level clearly identified as the Caldicott guardian with responsibility for promoting confidentiality within the organisation. It remains however a matter of both the law and professional practice that each and every individual health professional is personally and professionally accountable for their actions and this includes their decisions in relation to the disclosure of confidential information.

Reference

Bristol Royal Infirmary (2001) *Learning from Bristol: the Report of the Public Inquiry into Children's Heart Surgery at the Bristol Royal Infirmary 1984–1995*. Command Paper CM 5207 July 2001; http://www.bristol-inquiry.org.uk/.

Table of cases

Table of statutes

Abbreviations

ACAS	Advisory, Conciliation and Arbitration Service
ACOP	Approved Code of Practice
ACPC	Area Child Protection Committee:
AHP	Allied Health Professions
BCMA	British Complementary Medicine Association
CAFCASS	Child and Family Court Advisory and Support Service
CAM	complementary and alternative medicine
CDRP	Crime and Disorder Reduction Partnerships
CHAI	Commission of Healthcare Audit and Inspection
CHC	Community Health Council
CHI	Commission for Health Improvement
CHRE	Council for Healthcare Regulatory Excellence
CNHC	Complementary and Natural Healthcare Council
CNST	Clinical Negligence Scheme for Trusts
COPE	Committee on Publication Ethics
COREC	Central Office for Research Ethics Committees
COSHH	Control of Substances Hazardous to Health
COT	College of Occupational Therapists
CPA	care programme approach;
	comprehensive performance assessment
CPD	continuing professional development
CPPH	Commission for Patient and Public Involvement in Health
CPR	Civil Procedure Rules
CPS	Crown Prosecution Service
CRB	Criminal Records Bureau
CSCI	Commission for Social Care Inspection
DfES	Department for Education and Skill
DISC	Disability and Information Centre
DNR	do not resuscitate
DH	Department of Health
DOLS	Deprivation of Liberty Safeguards
DSS	Department of Social Security

EC	European Community
ECC	Ethics and Confidentiality Committee
EHR	electronic health record
EPR	electronic patient record
ESCR	electronic social care records
EWG	external working group
FHSA	family health services authorities
GDC	General Dental Council
GMC	General Medical Council
GSCC	General Social Care Council
HAI	hospital acquired infection
HASAW	Health and Safety at Work Act 1974
HIS	hospital information system
HPC	Health Professions Council
HRDG	Health Records and Data Protection Review Group
HSC	Health and Safety Commission
HSE	Health and Safety Executive
IBB	Independent Barring Board
ICAS	Independent Complaints and Advice Services
ICES	Integrated Community Equipment Services
ICP	integrated care pathways
IM&T	information management and technology
ISA	Independent Safeguarding Authority
JP	Justice of the Peace
LA	local authority
LINKS	Local Involvement Networks
LREC	Local Research Ethics Committee
MCA	Medicines Control Agency
MDA	Medical Devices Agency
MHAC	Mental Health Act Commission (replaced by CQC)
MHRA	Medicines and Healthcare Products Regulatory Agency (replacing MCA)
MHRT	Mental Health Review Tribunal
MREC	Multi-Centre Research Ethics Committee
NAI	non-accidental injury

NAO	National Audit Office
NCSC	National Care Standards Commission
NHSE	National Health Service Executive
NHSLA	National Health Service Litigation Authority
NICE	National Council for Health and Clinical Excellence
NIGB	National Information Governance Board for Health and Social Care
NMC	Nursing and Midwifery Council
NPSA	National Patient Safety Agency
NSF	National Service Frameworks
OT	occupational therapist/occupational therapy
PALS	Patient Advocacy and Liaison Service
PCMH	Plea and Case Management Hearing
PCT	Primary Care Trust
POVA	Protection of Vulnerable Adults
PVC	persistent vegetative state
REC	Research Ethics Committee
RIDDOR 95	Reporting of Injuries, Diseases and Dangerous Occurrences (Regulations) 1995
RMO	responsible medical officer
RPST	Risk Pooling Schemes for Trusts
SHA	strategic health authority
SOAD	second opinion appointed doctor
SRSC	Safety Representatives and Safety Committees (Regulations)
SSD	social services department
SSI	Social Services Inspectorate
VBS	Vetting and Barring Scheme

Glossary

accusatorial	a system of court proceedings where the two sides contest the issues (contrast with inquisitorial)
Act	of Parliament, statute
Actionable *per se*	a court action where the claimant does not have to show loss, damage or harm to obtain compensation, e.g. an action for trespass to the person
actus reus	the essential element of a crime which must be proved to secure a conviction, as opposed to the mental state of the accused (*mens rea*)
adversarial	the approach adopted in an accusatorial system
advocate	a person who pleads for another: it could be paid and professional, such as a barrister or solicitor, or it could be a lay advocate either paid or unpaid
assault	a threat of unlawful contact (trespass to the person)
balance of probabilities	the standard of proof in civil proceedings
barrister	a lawyer qualified to take a case in court
battery	an unlawful touching (see trespass to the person)
Bolam Test	The test laid down by Judge McNair in the case of *Bolam v. Friern HMC* on the standard of care expected of a professional in cases of alleged negligence
burden of proof	the duty of a party to litigation to establish the facts, or in criminal proceedings the duty of the prosecution to establish both the *actus reus* and the *mens rea*
cause of action	the facts that entitle a person to sue
civil action	proceedings brought in the civil courts
civil wrong	an act or omission which can be pursued in the civil courts by the person who has suffered the wrong (see torts)
committal proceedings	hearings before the magistrates to decide if a person should be sent for trial in the crown court
common law	law derived from the decisions of judges, case law, judge made law
conditional fee system	a system whereby client and lawyer can agree that payment of fees is dependent upon the outcome of the court action.
coroner	a person appointed to hold an inquiry (inquest) into a death in unexpected or unusual circumstances
criminal wrong	an act or omission which can be pursued in the criminal courts

damages	a sum of money awarded by a court as compensation for a tort or breach of contract
declaration	a ruling by the court, setting out the legal situation
dissenting judgment	A judge who disagrees with the decision of the majority of judges. distinguished (of cases) The rules of precedent require judges to follow decisions of judges in previous cases, where these are binding upon them. However in some circumstances it is possible to come to a different decision because the facts of the earlier case are not comparable to the case now being heard, and therefore the earlier decision can be 'distinguished'.
ex gratia	as a matter of favour, e.g. without admission of liability, of payment offered to a claimant
expert witness	evidence given by a person whose general opinion based on training or experience is relevant to some of the issues in dispute
hierarchy	the recognised status of courts which results in lower courts following the decisions of higher courts (see precedent). Thus decisions of the House of Lords must be followed by all lower courts unless, they can be distinguished (see above)
indictment	a written accusation against a person, charging him with a serious crime, triable by jury
injunction	an order of the court restraining a person
inquisitorial	a system of justice whereby the truth is revealed by an inquiry into the facts conducted by the judge e.g. coroner's court
judicial review	an application to the High Court for a judicial or administrative decision to be reviewed and an appropriate order made: e.g. declaration
litigation	civil proceedings
magistrate	a person (Justice of the Peace or stipendiary magistrate) who hears summary (minor) offences or indictable offences which can be heard in the magistrates court
mens rea	the mental element in a crime (contrasted with *actus reus*)
ombudsman	A Commissioner (e.g. health, Local Government) appointed by the Government to hear complaints
plaintiff	term formerly used to describe one who brings an action in the civil courts. Now the term claimant is used.
practice direction	guidance issued by the head of the court to which they relate on the procedure to be followed

precedent	a decision which may have to be followed in a subsequent court hearing (see hierarchy)
prima facie	at first sight, or sufficient evidence brought by one party to require the other party to provide a defence.
privilege	in relation to evidence, being able to refuse to disclose it to the court
proof	evidence which secures the establishment of a claimant's or prosecution's or defendant's case.
prosecution	the pursuing of criminal offences in court.
quantum	the amount of compensation, or the monetary value of a claim
reasonable doubt	to secure a conviction in criminal proceedings the prosecution must establish beyond reasonable doubt the guilt of the accused
Re F ruling	a professional who acts in the best interests of an incompetent person who is incapable of giving consent, does not act unlawfully if he follows the accepted standard of care according to the Bolam Test. (Now replaced by the Mental Capacity Act 2005)
solicitor	a lawyer who is qualified on the register held by the Law Society
statute law (statutory)	law made by Acts of Parliament
strict liability	liability for a criminal act where the mental element does not have to be proved; in civil proceedings liability without establishing negligence
subpoena	An order of the court requiring a person to appear as a witness (subpoena ad testificandum) or to bring records/ documents (subpoena duces tecum)
summary offence	a lesser offence which can only be heard by magistrates
tort	a civil wrong excluding breach of contract. It includes: negligence, trespass (to the person, goods or land), nuisance, breach of statutory duty and defamation.
trespass to the person	a wrongful direct interference with another person. Harm does not have to be proved.
ultra vires	Outside the powers given by law (e.g. of a statutory body or company)
vicarious liability	the liability of an employer for the wrongful acts of an employee committed whilst in the course of employment

Department of Health HSC 2000/009 and Data Protection Act 1998

Protection and Use of Patient Information which contains Schedules 1, 2 and 3 Data Protection Act 1998

Schedule 2 – conditions relevant for the purposes of the first principle: processing of any personal data

1. The data subject has given his consent to the processing.
2. The processing is necessary –
   a) for the performance of a contract to which the data subject is a party, or
   b) for the taking of steps at the request of the data subject with a view to entering into a contract.
3. The processing is necessary for compliance with any legal obligation to which the data controller is subject, other than an obligation imposed by contract.
4. The processing is necessary to protect the vital interests of the data subject.
5. The processing is necessary –
   for the administration of justice
   for the exercise of any functions conferred on any person by or under any enactment
   for the exercise of any functions of the Crown, a Minister of the Crown or government department
   for the exercise of any other functions of a public nature exercised in the public interest by any person.

6. (i)   The processing is necessary for the purpose of legitimate interests pursued by the data controller or by the third party or parties to whom the data are disclosed, except where the processing is unwarranted in any particular case by reason or prejudice to the rights and freedoms or legitimate interests of the data subject.

(ii) The Secretary of State may by order specify particular circumstances in which this condition is, or is not, to be taken to be satisfied.

Section C

Schedule 3 – Conditions relevant for the purposes of the first principle: processing of sensitive personal data

1. The data subject has given his explicit consent to the processing of the personal data.

2. (i)   The processing is necessary for the purposes of exercising or performing any right or obligation which is conferred or imposed by law on the data controller in connection with employment.

(ii) the Secretary of State may by order –
    a) exclude the application of sub-paragraph (1) in such cases as may be specified, or
    b) provide that, in such cases as may be specified, the condition in sub-paragraph (1) is not to be regarded as satisfied unless such further conditions as may be specified in the order are also satisfied.

3.1 The processing is necessary –
    a) in order to protect the vital interests of the data subject or another person, in a case where
        (i)   consent cannot be given by or on behalf of the data subject, or,
        (ii) the data controller cannot reasonably be expected to obtain the consent of the data subject, or
    b) in order to protect the vital interests of another person, in a case where consent by or on behalf of the data subject has been unreasonably withheld.

4. The processing –
    is carried out in the course of its legitimate activities by any body or association with
    is not established or conducted for profit, and
    exists for political, philosophical, religious or trade-union purposes,

is carried out with appropriate safeguards for the rights and freedoms of data subjects

relates only to individuals who either are members of the body or association or have regular contact with it in connection with its purposes, and

does not involve disclosure of the personal data to a third party without the consent of the data subject.

5. The information contained in the personal data has been made public as a result of steps deliberately taken by the data subject.

6. The processing –

is necessary for the purpose of, or in connection with, any legal proceedings (including prospective legal proceedings),

is necessary for the purpose of obtaining legal advice, or

is otherwise necessary for the purposes of establishing, exercising or defending legal rights.

7. (1) The processing is necessary –

for the administration of justice,

for the exercise of any functions conferred on any person by or under an enactment, or

for the exercise of any functions of the Crown, a Minister of the Crown or a government department

(2) The Secretary of State may by order –

exclude the application of sub-paragraph (1) in such cases as may be specified, or

provide that, in such cases as may be specified, the condition in sub-paragraph (1) is not to be regarded as satisfied unless such further conditions as may be specified in the order are also satisfied.

8. (1) The processing is necessary for medical purposes and is undertaken by–

a health professional, or

a person who in the circumstances owes a duty of confidentiality which is equivalent to that which would arise if that person were a health professional.

(2) In this paragraph 'medical purposes' includes the purposes of preventative medicine, medical diagnosis, medical research, the provision of care and treatment and the management of healthcare services.

9 (1) The processing –

is of sensitive personal data consisting of information as to racial or ethnic origin

is necessary for the purpose of identifying or keeping under review the existence or absence of equality of opportunity or treatment between persons of different racial or ethnic origins, with a view to enabling such equality to be promoted or maintained, and is carried out with appropriate safeguards for the rights and freedoms of data subjects.

(2) The Secretary of State may by order specify circumstances in which processing falling within sub-paragraph (1)(a) and (b) is, or is not, to be taken for the purposes of sub-paragraph (1)(c) to be carried out with the appropriate safeguards for the rights and freedoms of data subjects.

10. The personal data are processed in circumstances specified in an order made by the Secretary of State for the purposes of this paragraph.

Data Protection Act 1998 Department of Health guidance on Data Protection (Subject Access Modification) (Health) Order Statutory Instrument 2000 No 413

Part 3 – Rights of access to personal data

Access rights

1. In general the Act gives data subjects rights to access personal data about themselves which is held in either computerised or manual form, whenever the record was compiled.
2. The rights give an entitlement to:
   be informed whether personal data is processed (which includes being held or stored)
   a description of the data held, the purposes for which it is processed and to whom the data may be disclosed
   a copy of the information constituting the data
   information as to the source of the data.
2.1 Data subjects have access rights to all records irrespective of when they were created (whereas the Access to Health Records 1990 restricted access to records compiled after 1 November 1991).
3. There are exemptions to these rights:
   a request can be refused if the data controller is not supplied with the fee (see below) and such information as he may reasonably require to sat-

isfy himself as to the identity of the applicant and locate the information requested;

where information is processed solely for historical or scientific (including medical) research purposes, is not processed to support measures or decisions with respect to particular individuals nor in such a way as will or may cause substantial damage or distress to any data subject, and where the results will not be made available in a form from which individuals can be identified;

where disclosing the personal data would reveal information which relates to and identifies another person (for example that a relative had provided certain information) unless that person has consented to the disclosure or it is reasonable to comply with the request without that consent. The factors listed in section 7(6) should be considered in determining whether it would be reasonable in all the circumstances. These provisions do not apply where the person to be identified is a health professional who has either compiled or contributed to either the record or the care of the patient;

in the case of personal data consisting of information about the physical or mental health or condition of the data subject (i.e. most information held by NHS bodies) the Data Protection (Subject Access Modification) (Health) Order 2000 provides exemptions from the subject access rights in two situations:

where permitting access to the data would be likely to cause serious harm to the physical or mental health or condition of the data subject or any other person (which may include a health professional);

where the request for access is made by another on behalf of the data subject, such as a parent for a child, access can be refused if the data subject had either provided the information in the expectation it would not be disclosed to the applicant or had indicated it should not be so disclosed, or if the data was obtained as a result of any examination or investigation to which the data subject consented on the basis that information would not be so disclosed.

4. Before deciding whether the exemption in paragraph 3 iv (a) above applies, a data controller who is not a health professional must consult the health professional responsible for the clinical care of the data subject; or if there is more than one, the most suitable available health professional. If there is none, or the relevant data concern certain social security matters specified in Article 2(c)(ii) of the Order, a health professional with the necessary qualifications and experience to advise on the matters to which the information requested relates must be consulted.

Responding to access requests

5. A request for access must be made in writing, and no reason need be given. Subject to any applicable exemption, the applicant must be given a copy of the information and, where the data is not readily intelligible, an explanation (e.g. of abbreviations or medical terminology). Data controllers may not charge for the explanation, but can charge a fee for the application and copying charges.

5.1 Regulations on subject access fees have been agreed up until 24 October 2001 and are publicly available on the Home Office website at: http//www.homeoffice.gov.uk/ccpd/dpsafmsi.htm. The regulations provide that a maximum fee of £50 can be charged for access to health records for a transitional period running until 24 October 2001.

5.2 The data controller is entitled to satisfy itself that the applicant is either the data subject, or, if the applicant is applying on behalf of a data subject that the person has been authorised to do so.

5.3 The obligation to provide a copy may be waived where the data subject agrees otherwise or it is not possible to supply a copy of the material sought, or to do so would involve disproportionate effort (for example because papers have been destroyed, or are spread around the country).

5.4 However, the person may not wish to access their entire record and therefore NHS bodies may wish to confirm what material the applicant requires before processing the request which will both decrease the cost of copying for the applicant and unnecessary work by staff.

5.5 The Act does not provide an express right to directly inspect records, although it is permitted with the agreement of the data subject and data controller. It remains Department of Health policy that such requests should be accommodated subject to the exemptions listed in paragraph 3 above.

5.6 Requests for access should be responded to promptly, and no later than forty days after the request and fee (and any additional information as to the identity of the applicant or the location of the information reasonably required by the data controller) are received by the data controller. In exceptional circumstances if compliance is not possible within this period the applicant should be advised accordingly.

5.7 Where an access request has previously been complied with, the Act permits data controllers not to respond to a subsequent identical or similar request unless a reasonable interval has elapsed since the previous compliance. There is no definition of 'reasonable interval', but regard should be had to the nature of the data, how often it is altered and the reason for its processing. The reason for the request(s) may also be relevant.

Rights of rectification

6. If the data subject believes that data recorded about them are inaccurate the person may apply to the court, for an order, or to the DPC for an enforcement notice, either of which may require that the inaccurate data, and any expression of opinion based on it, is rectified, blocked, erased or destroyed.

7. However, where the data is inaccurate but accurately records information given by the data subject or another person the Court or the Commissioner may instead order that the record should be supplemented by a statement of the true facts as approved by the court/Commissioner.

Websites

Action for Advocacy	www.actionforadvocacy.org
Action on Elder Abuse	www.elderabuse.org.uk
Advisory Conciliation and Arbitration Service	www.acas.org.uk
Age Concern	www.ageconcern.org.uk
Alert	www.donoharm.org.uk
Alzheimer's Research	www.Alzheimers-research.org.uk
Alzheimer's Society	www.alzheimers.org.uk
ASA Advice	www.advice.org.uk
Association of Contentious Trust and Probate Solicitors	www.actaps.com
Audit Commission	www.audit-commission.gov.uk
Bailii (case law resource)	www.bailii.org/ew/cases
CARERS UK	www.carersonline.org.uk
	www.carersuk.org
Care Quality Commission	www.cqc.org.uk
Care Services Improvement Partnership	www.csip.org.uk
Citizens Advice Bureaux	www.citizensadvice.org.uk
Citizen Advocacy Information and Training	www.citizenadvocacy.org.uk
Civil Procedure Rules	www.open.gov.uk/lcd/civil/procrules_fin/crules.htm
Clinical Negligence Scheme for Trusts	www.nhsla.com/Claims/Schemes/CNST/
Commission for Racial Equality	www.cre.gov.uk
Commission for Social Care and Inspection	www.csci.gov.uk
Community Legal Service Direct	www.clsdirect.org.uk
Complementary Healthcare Information Service	www.chisuk.org.uk
Contact the Elderly	www.contact-the-elderly.org

Convention on the International Protection of Adults	www.hcch.net/index_en.php?
Council for Healthcare Regulatory Excellence	www.chre.org.uk
Commission for Patient and Public Involvement in Health	www.cppih.org
Counsel and Care	www.counselandcare.org.uk
Court Funds Office	www.hmcourts-service.gov.uk/ infoabout/cfo/index.htm
Court of Protection	via the Office of Public Guardian or HM Courts Services
Central Office for Research Ethics Committees	www.corec.org.uk
Dementia Care Trust	www.dct.org.uk
Department for Business Enterprise and Regulatory Reform	www.berr.gov.uk/employment
Department for Education and Skills	www.dfes.gov.uk
Department for Work and Pensions	www.dwp.gov.uk
Department of Health	www.dh.gov.uk
Department of Trade and Industry	www.dti.gov.uk
Disability Law Service	www.dls.org.uk
Domestic Violence	www.domesticviolence.gov.uk
Down's Syndrome Association	www.downs-syndrome.org.uk www.dsa-uk.com
Equality and Human Rights Commission	www.equalityhumanrights.com
Family Carer Support Service	www.familycarers.org.uk
Family Mediation Helpline	www.familymediationhelpline.co.uk
Foundation for People with Learning Disabilities	www.learningdisabilities.org.uk
General Medical Council	www.gmc-uk.org
Headway – Brain Injury Association	www.headway.org.uk
Health and Safety Commission	www.hsc.gov.uk
Health and Safety Executive	www.hse.gov.uk
Help the Aged	www.helptheagedorg.uk
Help the Hospices	www.hospiceinformation.info
Healthcare Commission	www.healthcarecommission.org.uk

Health Professions Council	www.hc-uk.org
HM Courts Service	www.hmcourts-service.gov.uk
Home Farm Trust	www.hft.org.uk
Human Fertilisation and Embryology Authority	www.hfea.gov.uk
Human Genetics Commission	www.hgc.gov.uk
Human Rights	www.humanrights.gov.uk
Independent Mental Capacity Advocate	www.dh.gov.uk.imca
Information Commissioner's Office	www.ico.gov.uk
Independent Safeguarding Authority	www.isa-gov.org.uk
Law Centres Federation	www.lawcentres.org.uk
Law Society	www.lawsociety.org.uk choosingandusing/findingasolicitor.law
Legal cases (England and Wales)	www.bailli.org/ew/cases
Legislation	www.opsi.gov.uk/legislation or www. legislation.hmso.gov.uk
Linacre Centre for Healthcare Ethics	www.linacre.org
Making Decisions Alliance	www.makingdecisions.org.uk
Manic Depression Fellowship	www.mdf.org.uk
MedicAlert Foundation	www.medicalert.org.uk
Medicines and Healthcare Products Regulatory Agency	www.mhra.gov.uk
MENCAP	www.mencap.org.uk
Mental Capacity Implementation Programme	www.dca.go.uk/legal-policy/mental-capacity/index.htm
Mental Health Act Commission	www.mhac.org.uk
Mental Health Foundation	www.mentalhealth.org.uk
Mental Health Lawyers Association	www.mhla.co.uk
Mental Health Matters	www.mentalhealthmatters.com
Mind	www.mind.org.uk
Ministry of Justice	www.justice.gov.uk
Motor Neurone Disease Association	www.mndassociation.org.uk
National Audit Office	www.nao.gov.uk
National Autistic Society	www.nas.org.uk www.autism.org.uk

National Care Association	www.nca.gb.com
National Family Carer Network	www.familycarers.org.uk
National Health Service Litigation Authority	www.nhsla.com
National Information and Governance Board for Health and Social Care	www.nigb.nhs.uk
National Mediation Helpline	www.nationalmediationhelpline.com
National Patient Safety Agency	www.npsa.gov.uk
National Perinatal Epidemiology Unit	www.npeu.ox.ac.uk
National Treatment Agency	www.nta.nhs.uk
NHS website	www.nhs.uk
NHS Direct	www.nhsdirect.nhs.uk
NHS Institute for Innovation and Improvement	www.institute.nhs.uk
NHS Professionals	www.nhsprofessionals.nhs.uk
NICE	www.nice.org.uk
Nursing and Midwifery Council	www.nmc-uk.org
Office of Public Guardian	www.guardianship.gov.uk
Office of Public Sector Information	www.opsi.gov.uk
Official Solicitor	www.officialsolicitor.gov.uk
Open Government	www.open.gov.uk
Pain website	www.pain-talk.co.uk
Patient's Association	www.patients-association.org.uk
Patient Concern	www.patientconcern.org.uk
People First	www.peoplefirst.org.uk
Prevention of Professional Abuse Network	www.popan.org.uk
Princess Royal Trust for Carers	www.carers.org
Relatives and Residents Association	www.releres.org
RESCARE (The National Society for mentally disabled people in residential care)	www.rescare.org.uk
Respond	www.respond.org.uk
Rethink (formerly the National Schizophrenia Fellowship)	www.rethink.org
Royal College of Nursing	www.rcn.org.uk
Royal College of Psychiatrists	www.rcpsych.ac.uk

SANE	www.sane.org.uk
Scope	www.scope.org.uk
Sense	www.sense.org.uk
Solicitors for the Elderly	www.solicitorsfortheelderly.com
Speaking Up	www.speakingup.org
Speakability	www.speakability.org.uk
Shipman Inquiry	www.the-shipman-inquiry.org.uk/ reports.asp
Solicitors for the Elderly	www.solicitorsfortheelderly.com
Stroke Association	www.stroke.org.uk
Together: Working for Wellbeing	www.together-uk.org
Turning Point	www.turning-point.co.uk
UK Homecare Association	www.ukhca.co.uk
UK Parliament	www.parliament.uk
United Response	www.unitedresponse.org.uk
Values into Action	www.viauk.org
Veterans Agency	www.veteransagency.org.uk
VOICE UK	www.voiceuk.clara.net
Voluntary Euthanasia Society	www.ves.org.uk
Welsh Assembly Government	www.wales.gov.uk
World Medical Association	www.wma.net/e/policy/b3.htm

Further reading

Carey, P. (2004) *Data Protection: a Practical Guide to UK and EU Law*, 2nd edn. Oxford University Press, Oxford.

Dimond, B. C. (1999) *Patients Rights, Responsibilities and the Nurse*, 2nd edn. Quay Books, London.

Dimond, B. C. (2009) *Legal Aspects of Consent*, 2nd edn Quay Books, London.

Dimond, B. C. (2010) *Legal Aspects of Nursing*, 6th edn. Prentice Hall, London.

Foster, C. and Peacock, N. (2000) *Clinical Confidentiality*. Monitor Press, Sudbury.

Hendrick, J. (2006) *Law and Ethics in Nursing and Healthcare*, 2nd edn. Nelson Thornes, London.

Herring, J. (2006) *Medical Law and Ethics*. Oxford University Press, Oxford.

Jones, M. A. (2007*) Textbook on Torts*, 9th edn. Oxford University Press, Oxford.

Jones, M. A. and Morris, A. E. (2005) *Blackstone's Statutes on Medical Law*, 4th edn. Oxford University Press, Oxford.

Kennedy, I. and Grubb, A. (2000) *Medical Law and Ethics*, 3rd edn. Butterworth, London.

Leathard, A. and McLaren, S. (eds.) (2007) *Ethics: Contemporary Challenges in Health and Social Care*. Policy Press, Bristol.

Leigh-Pollit, P. and Mullock, J. (2001) *The Data Protection Act Explained*, 3rd edn. The Stationery Office, London.

McHale, J. and Fox, M. (2007) *Health Care Law*, 2nd edn. Sweet & Maxwell, London.

McHale, J. and Tingle, J. (2007) *Law and Nursing*, 2nd edn. Elsevier Health Sciences, London.

Maclean, A. (2001) *Briefcase of Medical Law*. Cavendish, London.

Montgomery, J. (2003) *Health Care Law*, 2nd edn. Oxford University Press, Oxford.

Stauch, M. (2005) *Text and Materials on Medical Law*, 3rd edn. Cavendish, London.

Tingle, J. and Cribb, A. (2007) *Nursing Law and Ethics*, 3rd edn. Blackwell Publishers, Oxford.

Warnock, M. (2002) *An Intelligent Person's Guide to Ethics*. Duckworths, London.

Watt, H. (2000) *Life and Death in Healthcare Ethics – a Short Introduction*. Routledge, London.

White, R., Carr, P. and Lowe, N. (2002) *A Guide to the Children Act 1989*, 3rd edn. Butterworth, London.

Wilkinson, R. and Caulfield, H. (2000) *The Human Rights Act: a Practical Guide for Nurses*. Whurr Publishers, London.

Zander, M. (2005) *Police and Criminal Evidence Act*, 1st supplement to 5th edn. Sweet & Maxwell, London.

Index